This book is given
In honor of
Maria Pindicblaj
by
Florin & Lidiana Pindicblaj
May 2001

Shakespeare AND THE

POLITICS OF CULTURE

IN LATE VICTORIAN ENGLAND

Linda Rozmovits

Shakespeare AND THE

POLITICS OF CULTURE

IN LATE VICTORIAN ENGLAND

THE JOHNS HOPKINS

UNIVERSITY PRESS

BALTIMORE AND LONDON

The Johns Hopkins University Press

2715 North Charles Street

Baltimore, Maryland 21218-4363

The Johns Hopkins Press Ltd.,

London

www.press.jhu.edu

Library of Congress
Cataloging-in-Publication Data
will be found at the end of this book.
A catalog record for this
book is available from the British Library.

ISBN 0-8018-5836-4

For my parents

Contents

Acknowledgments

I would like to express my gratitude to the Social Sciences and Humanities Research Council of Canada for funding this research.

I was considerably assisted in my work by librarians at the Institute for Studies in Education, the Jewish Studies Library at the University of London, and the University of Sussex Library, where a particular debt of gratitude is owed to Bet Inglis and Ian Budden. Claire Hudson of the Theatre Museum was exceptionally kind and helpful on very short notice.

David Alderson, John Barrell, Carol Dyhouse, Esther Frank, Sue Gardner, Geoff Hemstedt, Marcia Pointon, Zailig Pollock, Louise Purbrick, Lindsay Smith, and Norman Vance were extremely generous in sharing their time and their ideas.

My colleagues at the University of East London have been unfailing in their support, but Alan O'Shea, especially, has been there above and beyond the call of duty.

Citations and Abbreviations

References follow the MLA conventions for in-text citation. Un-signed newspaper or journal articles are referred to by the title of the publication in which they appear and the date. *Theatre* 1/3/80, for example, refers to the item listed in the bibliography as "Our Omnibus-Box," *Theatre,* 1 March 1880, 188. All such unsigned articles appear together in a separate section of the bibliography.

All references to the text of *The Merchant of Venice* are to the New Penguin edition (ed. W. Moelwyn Merchant [1967]).

The titles of the following publications have been abbreviated as given here for in-text references:

GOP	*Girl's Own Paper*
MV	*The Merchant of Venice,* as presented at the Lyceum The-atre, under the Management of Henry Irving (London: Chiswick P, 1881)
PP	Parliamentary Papers
SSL	C. H. Firth, *Sir Sidney Lee,* from the Proceedings of the British Academy, vol. 15 (London: Humphrey Milford, n.d. [1929])

Shakespeare AND THE

POLITICS OF CULTURE

IN LATE VICTORIAN ENGLAND

Introduction

While contemporary anxieties about race and moral relativism have relegated *The Merchant of Venice* to the second division of Shakespearian drama, throughout the late nineteenth and early twentieth centuries (roughly speaking from about the 1870s to the 1920s), the play was considered to represent the height of Shakespeare's achievement. In 1925 Geoffrey Crump, in his *Guide to the Study of Shakespeare's Plays,* articulated a view of *The Merchant* which, although largely forgotten by us, had by that time predominated for more than a half-century. In *The Merchant of Venice,* he wrote, "Shakespeare was . . . trying to imagine an ideal community after his own heart, where everyone thought first of the good of everyone else." "It is the happiest of Shakespeare's plays," Crump declared, and "one can well believe that he loved writing it" (64–65):

> Though Shakespeare afterward wrote many other plays
> of equal and greater value as drama, he never wrote
> another that was so full of exquisite lyrical poetry, nor
> one in which the level of grace and beauty was so unfail-
> ingly sustained in such qualities as wealth of language,
> perfection of imagery, rhythm, and charm of imagina-
> tion. This, after all, is only what we expect if we believe
> it to be Shakespeare's consciously happiest play . . . He
> could not have written such a play either in the inexperi-
> ence and immaturity of his youth or in the sophistica-
> tion and bitterness of his later years. (66)

Affirming Crump's analysis, school and popular editions of *The Merchant of Venice* consistently advertised its charms as one of the greatest and most unadulteratedly happy works of English literature. It was reckoned to be "one of the best known and best liked plays in English" (Maltby 7), part of the "sunshine of . . . [Shakespeare's] drama" (Meiklejohn 1), and "giv[ing] a brighter view of life [and] show[ing] man striving against the difficulties which beset him, and ultimately triumphant" (Blackie's vi).

Even beyond this general celebration of the play's life-affirming qualities, its immense popularity in pedagogical circles was attributed to its perceived value to both pupils and teachers. On the one hand, *The Merchant* was considered to be accessible; as one of Shakespeare's "easier plays" (Board of Education, *Suggestions* 20), it was declared to be one of the texts "most naturally absorbed and enjoyed by children" of eleven or twelve years of age (Polkinghorne and Polkinghorne 225). Thus, it enjoyed a reputation not simply as a *great* play but as a *first* play, which is to say as the preferred vehicle for a child's induction into the serious study of literature. On the other hand, despite its accessibility, it was a text from which modern educators clearly felt they could wrest the full value of literary study. When F. H. Hayward, inspector of schools under the London County Council, produced a text on *The Primary Curriculum*, it was *The Merchant of Venice* he chose to illustrate the practical method for making the connection between "Literature and Moral Instruction" (57) and for fulfilling such pedagogical imperatives as the "Elucidation of Meaning, and 'Teaching to Think' in a Literature Lesson" (49).

An even more substantive endorsement of *The Merchant of Venice* was offered by the English Association in a pamphlet entitled *The Teaching of Shakespeare in Secondary Schools.* Here it was noted that "the plays suitable for study between the ages of 12 and 14"—which is, to restate a crucial point, at the initiation of a child's institutional relationship to Shakespeare—"are limited in number, the themes of many being beyond the pupils' experience and range of understanding" (1). In order to preempt inappropriate choices of what were then euphemistically designated "adult" plays, the association prescribed a list of plays suitable for young readers as well as the order in which they ought to be studied. On the list of preferred texts *The Merchant of Venice* is second only to *Julius Caesar,* the play with which it sometimes alternated in its status as perennial favorite and whose great popularity was clearly attributable to the fact that it was perceived "by British audiences of the day as the direct analogue to imperial Britain" (Berry 154).[1]

Yet, while the extraordinary popularity of *The Merchant of Venice* within educational circles is thus evident, by no means was this popularity limited to the pedagogical sphere or its significance circumscribed by debates about educational utility. On the London stage Henry Irving redefined popularity with a production of *The Merchant* which broke all existing box office records, was the staple of his revival and touring repertoire for decades to come, and which has since come to occupy a central place in histories of the Victorian theater. Moreover, in the middle-class and popular press, even in children's magazines, *The Merchant* and its characters were frequently invoked as icons of social and political debate. Feminist and antifeminist campaigners alike sought to validate their respective causes by appealing to the example of Portia, while the figure of Shylock was taken up in countless ways in debates about the "Jewish question" from the 1870s onward.

In short, *The Merchant of Venice* might well be described as a late Victorian popular obsession. The play seemed to serve as a lens through which people filtered their experience of social life and social change, through which they negotiated their responses to events and developments that disturbed or excited them, and, on occasion, into which they sought to retreat from a society that was changing in ways they considered to be unmanageable, if not at times intolerable. The relationship between *The Merchant of Venice* and the people who studied it, read it, or watched it being performed, who had it quoted or misquoted to them, or who were affected by beliefs, policies, or laws that had somehow been influenced by it, was an extraordinarily dynamic one in England from the 1870s to the 1920s. It is this strange and dynamic relationship that this book will explore.

A number of historical issues figure prominently in the sorts of late-nineteenth- and early-twentieth-century responses to *The Merchant of Venice* with which this book is concerned. Roughly speaking, these cluster around the areas of educational reform, women's politics, and the Jewish question.

In the sphere of education the 1870s and the decades that followed

constituted a period marked by significant reforms: the modernization of the ancient universities, increased educational provision for
girls and women, the implementation of universal elementary education, and the expansion and modernization of the curriculum were
all now under way.[2] Mirroring these changes were a "dramatic in-
crease in cheap commercial publications and the arrival of mass-
circulation newspapers" (Lawson and Silver 326), in effect the print
vehicles that contributed so significantly to the circulation of *The
Merchant* itself as well as to the proliferation of scholarly and popular discourse about it. Simply put, more people were going to
school, staying there longer, and gaining exposure to the expanding
and modernized curriculum than had been the case prior to the
1870s. They were also more likely to include some form of reading as
part of their leisure-time activities than had been the case in the early
part of the century. Hence, the increased likelihood of a work of literature attaining the sort of widespread social currency that *The
Merchant of Venice* came to possess in the period.

At one level, then, the reform and expansion of educational provision contributed to the popularity of *The Merchant of Venice* by its
"democratization" of learning. But at another level the play's unprecedented popularity was equally linked to the underlying conser-
vatism associated with the modern curriculum. For the modern curriculum was not, of course, universally adopted, elite public schools
and the ancient universities, for the most part, holding fast to their
commitment to ancient traditions. The modern curriculum, it is now
well-known, was for those considered incapable of meeting the demands of Greek and Latin and for whom proficiency in complex science and mathematics would have been declared unattainable: colonial subjects, women, and the working classes.

While much of the revised curriculum was taken up with the study
of modern European languages, history, and elementary mathematics, as has often been noted, at its very heart was English literature, the so-called civilizing subject. In the colonies English was employed to foster deference to European culture, while at home it
aimed to mollify the increasingly militant working classes and to
secure the affections of women for long-standing English traditions,
values, and codes of social behavior.[3] Not surprisingly, Shakespeare,

the national poet, and such masterworks as *The Merchant of Venice*, were considered central to this enterprise.

Thus it was, in a sense, inevitable that, as a text so prominently placed within the modern curriculum and therefore within the sphere of female education, *The Merchant* would intersect with debates about the role of women in a number of ways. Predictably, the value of Shakespeare study for English women was articulated dominantly and conservatively through the discourses of Victorian femininity and civic maternalism which pervaded so much of the thinking around female education.[4] While on one level, then, Shakespeare was so aggressively appropriated by the proponents of Victorian femininity, his female characters held aloft as incarnations of its highest ideals, the association of Shakespeare and Victorian women had another, more unforeseen side. For, rather than simply reinforcing an attitude of submission, enhanced formal education led significant numbers of women to question the logic of acquiring skills beyond those needed for a strictly domestic existence, fostering desires for personal advancement, work outside the home, and a serious reconsideration of the institution of marriage. Among other things the period with which this book is concerned was, of course, the heyday of nineteenth-century feminism. To give it the appellation it eventually acquired, this was the era of the New Woman, and the reception of *The Merchant of Venice* in late Victorian society is closely interwoven with this fact.[5]

For conservatives and antifeminist campaigners alike Portia may have been an icon of Victorian femininity, but for advocates of gender political reform she became the New Woman incarnate. Wealthy and uncontrolled by either husband or father, learned, independent, dressed as a man and making her petition in a court of law, Portia held a magnetic attraction for those who aspired to the freedom she possessed. Indeed, the single most striking feature of many of the essays, articles, and schoolbooks in which her character is debated and assessed is the extent to which they construe *The Merchant of Venice* to be a play primarily about Portia, her wealth, her marriage, and her day in court. Without a doubt this is the aspect of the play's reception in the late nineteenth and early twentieth centuries which has been most obscured by the passage of time. Approaching the text in the late twentieth century, it is difficult to imagine a time when, for many, *The Merchant of Venice* was a play, first and foremost, about the marriage prospects of a wealthy orphaned young woman with a subplot about a Jewish moneylender hovering in the background.

Yet it would be misleading to suggest that the unexpected prominence of Portia, and that part of the text we have come to think of as the subplot, utterly dominated the late Victorian reception of *The Merchant of Venice*. Then, as now, Shylock and his demand for a pound of flesh commanded great attention, aroused strong passions, and became the subject of widespread and, at times, acrimonious debate. How could it be otherwise when the Jewish question was so prominent in people's minds?

From the time of their formal readmission to England in the seventeenth century to the repeal of political disabilities in 1858, the Anglo-Jewish community had been small, predominantly middle class, and largely willing and able to accommodate the demands set for its members' absorption into English society. But in the latter decades of the nineteenth and early years of the twentieth century that accommodation was disrupted, as the character of Anglo-Jewry changed dramatically in a number of ways.[6]

The British liberal state had invested significantly in an image of itself as different from many of its "intolerant" counterparts by virtue of its favorable treatment of its Jewish minority. By the 1880s, however, this claim was being sorely tested by the mass immigration of Jews from Eastern Europe. Within the space of a few decades the work of established Anglo-Jewry to achieve an inconspicuous place in English society was threatened by the mushrooming of a highly conspicuous and profoundly alien immigrant community. Toleration of a small, middle-class population that contributed significantly to the wealth of the nation had been relatively easy to achieve. But, as the testimonies of the social investigators suggest, extending this spirit of toleration to 150,000 foreign-looking destitute people, many of whom spoke no English, practiced strange religious customs, or exhibited unwelcome political tendencies, was altogether another matter.

At the other end of the spectrum the period covered by this book is also one in which Jews became conspicuous among the very

Finally, readers anticipating an account of the late Victorian *Merchant of Venice* as emblematic monolith of nineteenth-century anti-Semitism may be equally disappointed. For, while anti-Semitism was certainly prevalent within the culture, the relationship between anti-Jewish sentiment and *The Merchant of Venice* during the period could hardly be described as straightforward. In the first instance (as I have already indicated and as chap. 2 explores in detail) the text was, for many, primarily about Portia and not Shylock, a fact that in itself must encourage us to relinquish our long-standing assumptions about the play's *inevitable* meanings and its social role. Moreover, as I will demonstrate in chapter 3, the play, particularly under Henry Irving's direction, seems for a variety of reasons to have unleashed a culture of identification with Jews, if not one of overt sympathy for them. All this will, I hope, serve to underline the profoundly ambivalent nature of late Victorian England's relationship to its Jews. And one of my aims has thus been to preserve a sense of, rather than to explain away, these ambivalences and ambiguities.

In seeking to fulfill this aim, I have tried throughout the book, but with special emphasis in the final chapter, to be particularly attentive to narrative process and to the storytelling practices of a culture, because it is in those practices, I would argue, that the structures of social exclusion are simultaneously inscribed and undermined through the potency and instability of language.

On these grounds, among others, my starting point is therefore neither a long view of Shakespeare and the Jewish question, since this lends itself too much to the presumption that *The Merchant* is overwhelmingly, if not exclusively, a play of Jewish concern, nor a historical overview of the play itself, since surveys of this kind have the tendency to create ahistorical continuities at the expense of historically material differences.

Rather I have chosen to begin with bardolatry, the legendary culture of Victorian Shakespeare worship, because, if we are to appreciate *The Merchant*'s importance in late Victorian England, we need to understand something of Shakespeare's status, more generally, within that culture. For, ultimately, my aim is to lay the groundwork for understanding why it was that Shakespeare's *Merchant of Venice*, of all texts, came to loom as large as it did in the late Victorian social imagination.

The Word and the Book

In his allusion to the Deity, [Shakespeare] delights in those attributes
that . . . represent Him as the God of Love and Peace . . . rather . . .
recommend[ing] "the quality of mercy" than the rugged justice of
"the eye for eye and tooth for tooth" morality of the Hebrew Code
of Ethics.
—Charles Plumptre, "The Religion and Morality of Shakespeare's
Works"

Of all Bernard Shaw's infamous pronouncements about the theater,
perhaps none has been more enduring than that which gave us the
concept of bardolatry, the idolatrous worship of the bard, Shakespeare, by his legendarily impressionable and misguided public.[1] Indeed, the continuing resonance of the concept for modern criticism
has made it a centrally organizing one, both for critics of the conventional liberal scholarship that dominated Shakespeare studies as
late as the 1970s and for more recent writers, several of whom have
been concerned with the processes by which Shakespeare's status
as the bard was socially inscribed, particularly in the hundred-odd
years between 1660 and 1769, which is to say, between the Restoration and Garrick's Jubilee.[2] But what has at times been lost sight of
is the fact that, in terms of a history that begins in 1660, Shaw's remarks come rather late in the day, in 1901 in fact, and in the context
of a discussion clearly focused on the culture of the late Victorian
theater. This is by no means to dismiss Shaw's backward glance, in
the preface to *Plays for Puritans,* to the great age of Shakespeare adu-
lation through "improvement" but, rather, to caution against the
flattening-out effect of a scholarly perspective that, despite its oppo-
sition to liberal humanism, may inadvertently construct "unbroken
lines" of its own. What I am arguing about the concept of bardolatry, then, is that it is best understood not as a phenomenon that has
been fundamentally continuous over the last three hundred years
but as one that has been remarkable for the strikingly different in-
flections it has assumed at different times.

While it has long been a scholarly commonplace to refer to bardolatry as a pseudoreligious phenomenon, for example, with the char-

acterization being applied across a wide range of social contexts and historical moments, it is, in fact, only from about the 1860s onward that bardolatry *literally* assumes religious or quasi-religious forms. People in 1769 may have been energetically and publicly celebrating Shakespeare's importance as the national poet, but by 1869 assertions of Shakespeare's unique status had not only acquired a fiercely moral inflection (conspicuously absent in the profane celebrations of a century earlier) but, indeed, had come to inhabit forms of discussion, celebration, and worship which belonged not to any mortal man however accomplished but to God alone. Thus, one of my aims here is to provide a usefully detailed account of this more strictly limited phenomenon and to suggest something of how this form of pseudo-religion would have exerted its influence in a wider sphere in England from the mid nineteenth to the early twentieth centuries.

There is, however, another set of concerns which this chapter will seek to explore, and in setting these out it will be helpful, momentarily to return to Shaw's preface. The preface to *Plays for Puritans,* as I have already indicated, is largely taken up with Shaw's concerns about the late Victorian theater. But two elements within the preface call for particular attention here. One is the singling out at several points of Henry Irving as an icon of everything that, in Shaw's view, was wrong with late Victorian theatrical production: "gorgeous stage ritualism superimposed on reckless mutilations of . . . [the] text" (62). The other, somewhat more unexpectedly (for swipes at Irving were part of Shaw's stock-in-trade), is Shaw's allusion to what he evidently perceived to be a significant contest of influence being enacted not on the stage but in the audience between the traditional English middle-class occupants of the stalls and their burgeoning Jewish replacements. "The stalls cannot be fully understood," he wrote, "without taking into account the absence of the rich evangelical English merchant and his family, and the presence of the rich Jewish merchant and *his*" (60). While on the matter of the changing tastes in leading ladies, he remarked that "the stalls . . . were apt to insist on more Rebecca and less Rowena than the pit cared for" (63). The point, although it is somewhat tangentially made, is that the Jewish presence in the theater, like Irving's textual meddling and predilection for visual splendor, was part of a trend, under the "financier's influence," which meant that "the way is smoothest for those plays and those performers that appeal specially to the Jewish taste" (61). With these obvious echoes of *The Merchant* in mind, then, my second aim in taking bardolatry as my starting point for this cultural history of the play in the late Victorian period is to understand why it was that, within that culture of Shakespeare worship, it was the *Merchant of Venice*, above all, which came to be held in such esteem.

I

While it is David Garrick who is usually credited with fanning the flames of Shakespeare idolatry, his Jubilee of 1769 occupying center stage in the historiography of the practice,[3] there is reason to argue for the 1860s generally, and the 1864 tercentenary in particular, as an equally significant watershed in the history of Shakespeare as religion. For, though Garrick may have staged the first full-scale Shakespeare extravaganza and declared the bard to be "the God of our idolatry," the Stratford tercentenary of 1864 signaled a clear shift, in the history of bardolatry, away from Garrick's highly idiosyncratic, rhetorical style of celebration toward institutional structures and modes of behavior strongly associated with the formal conventions of Christian worship.

As part of its cumbersome bureaucracy, for example, the 1864 organization featured a conspicuous and high-profile clerical presence, including three bishops and scores of other notable clergy.[4] Furthermore, unlike Garrick's Jubilee, in which the only event to take place in church was a performance of Arne's *Judith* (whose relevance to Shakespeare was tenuous at best), the events of celebration week 1864 included a Sunday devoted entirely to worship at Holy Trinity Church, the highlights of which were the two Shakespeare sermons. These would become an annual tradition in churches all over the country, preached on the Sunday nearest Shakespeare's birthday, and were destined to underline the "coincidence" of Shakespeare's birthday, Saint George's Day, and the proximity of both to the most important date of the Christian calendar, especially in years in which Shakespeare Sunday fell in the week immediately after Easter. Moreover, it was in 1864 that we get the first recorded appearance of the pejorative *Shakspearolatry,* obvious predecessor to Shaw's retrospective coinage, and the related appearance of *Shakespeariana* the following year (OED).

On Shakespeare Sunday 1864, "the Revd. G. Granville presided over large congregations at 11 am and 3 pm" (Foulkes, *Tercentenary* 28) with the morning service going on until 2 P. M ., allowing only a brief interval for those who expected to attend the afternoon service as well. The morning sermon was delivered by Richard Chenevix Trench, archbishop of Dublin, and the afternoon sermon by Charles Wordsworth, bishop of Saint Andrews. In several respects the choice of preachers and the themes of their texts set out contemporary pre-occupations.

The first thing to note about both men was the way in which they combined their sacred callings with considerable accomplishments in the secular literary world, a combination increasingly characteristic of the period, in which the influence of the German "higher criticism" was being strongly felt in England. Trench "was a distinguished Biblical scholar, philologist—the instigator of the Oxford English Dictionary—, translator from Spanish, and a poet in his own right, having been a contemporary of Alfred Tennyson and Arthur Hallam at Cambridge" (Foulkes, *Tercentenary* 28). Wordsworth was the nephew of the famous poet and, in the same year as the tercentenary, author of *Shakspeare's Knowledge and Use of the Bible,* a book that was instrumental in promoting an outpouring of writings on similar themes. Trench's text was "Every good gift and every perfect gift is from above and cometh down from the Father of Light" (AV 1.17). Wordsworth had chosen "All Thy Works Praise Thee, O Lord" (Ps. 145.10).

As Richard Foulkes has argued, Trench's sermon can easily be read as "an object lesson in the Victorian establishment's desire to use Shakespeare to reinforce its own moral, social and political outlook" (*Tercentenary* 28). And, unquestionably, Trench's sermon contains several elements that support such a view: the emphasis on Shakespeare's morally sound healthy qualities, his tableau of exemplary women, his role as the national poet, but especially his definition of genius as an attribute wholly reconcilable with ordinariness, obedience, sober mindedness, and a contentedly domestic outlook. The same argument could easily be applied to Wordsworth's sermon, which similarly emphasizes Shakespeare's virtue, efficacy as the national poet, and importance as a spiritual antidote to Baconian scientism. But there is a great deal more to both these sermons and the new culture of Shakespeare as religion which they herald than just their obvious propaganda value, and I want to consider them closely in order to develop a more nuanced sense of the social context in which they were delivered and of what they were about.

To begin with Trench's sermon, the most striking thing about it, and certainly the attribute that confounds expectations about the readiness of all Victorians to exploit the conventional hyperbole about Shakespeare, is the obvious discomfort he felt at having been asked to deliver a sermon on Shakespeare at all, that is, at having been asked to apply a form of worship usually reserved for the supreme being to a mortal man, however sublime. "It has . . . been devised wisely and well," he began, "that the sermon of to-day should stand, if possible, in some connection with the celebrations which fill up the remainder of the week":

> You, who have sought that such a connection should exist, have thus declared many things. You have declared first, that you have no intention nor desire to separate the gift from the Giver . . . to make much of man at the expense of Him who is the God of man, and from whom [all?] wit, wisdom, intelligence, or goodness . . . originally came . . .
>
> It has then, doubtless, been well imagined that the sacred services of to-day . . . should yet blend themselves, as harmoniously they may, with the other more festal solemnities of the time. One thing only I could willingly have desired—namely, that on some other, less unequal to the occasion, had devolved the task of tracing the connection between them, and of weaving one into the other . . . I am not wholly unaware of the difficulties of my undertaking . . .
>
> Thus, if I *preach* about Shakespeare . . . you will remember that this is the very thing which I am set to do; which thus in my office as a minister of Christ, and

> in his holy house, I could alone consent to do. And . . .
> if I pass over innumerable aspects on which he presents
> himself to us, and contemplate him only upon one . . .
> the directly moral—it is not because others are indiffer-
> ent to me . . . but because here I have no right, as cer-
> tainly I have no desire, to contemplate him in any other
> aspect than this. (5–7)

Arguably, Trench's protestations of personal inadequacy, and his reluctance to get down to the task at hand, may be read as the sort of calculated false modesty one might expect on such a prestigious occasion. But, alternatively, the level of unease evident in his pro-tracted opening remarks suggests a genuine discomfort with the subject and the occasion. We may notice, for example, the way in which Trench repeatedly distanced himself from the endeavor, em-phasizing the contrived nature of the connection between a celebra-tion of Shakespeare the man and the practice of Christian worship. "It has . . . been *devised* wisely and well that the sermon of to-day *should stand, if possible,* in some connection with the celebrations which fill up the remainder of the week." "*You* who have *sought* that such a connection *should exist,* have thus declared many things." "It has . . . doubtless been *well imagined* that the sacred services of to-day . . . *should* . . . *blend themselves* . . . with the other . . . solemnities of the time" (my emph.). Evidently, Trench was anxious to convey the message that these were neither *his* devices nor *his* imaginings, a sentiment that is further underlined by his claim to being unequal to the task and, indeed, by his going so far as to wish aloud that some-one else had been asked to do the "tracing" and "weaving" of con-nections between the one and the other.

The point I am making here is not that this discomfort some-how negates a more conventional reading of the moral program of Trench's sermon, for once past the initial stumbling blocks it be-comes largely the sort of text one would expect. Rather, my point is that belying its Victorian conventionality is a powerful indication that the tremendous fad for writing, thinking, and talking about the relationship between Shakespeare and the Bible, which emerged in the 1860s and maintained its hold in England well into the 1920s, was not necessarily encouraged, or even strictly speaking approved of, by the church, no matter how firmly established and no matter how often the connections between Shakespeare, Saint George, and God the Creator were declared. For Trench was not alone in his discomfort.

Like his tercentenary counterpart, Charles Wordsworth was, repeatedly, at pains to emphasize the proper object of our adoration: not man the creative genius but God the Creator of man. "We are wont to speak of the works of Shakspeare," he wrote, "but never, never let us forget that the author of those works was himself a work of God . . . [and] in honouring our great poet, we shall be led to magnify God in him . . . and not only so, but to bless God for him, as an inestimably precious and most glorious gift" ("Sermon" 386). Similarly, R. W. Dale, a Congregationalist divine, also preaching a Shakespeare sermon in Stratford that day (though not as part of the official celebrations), was equally reluctant to move very far away from a note of caution. For, while he declared early on that it was not his intention to spend the evening reiterating that most basic tenet of Christian theology—namely, that in "doing homage to human genius it is well that we should remember that *Genius is the gift of God*" (4)—he seems to have found it hard to do anything else. "If God is the Author and Giver of all intellectual life, it is our duty to offer Him grateful praise while we are doing honour to genius" (7). "Who can estimate the magnitude of the blessing it was in God's heart to confer on the English people when He endowed our great poet with gifts so vast and rare?" (8). Our "intellectual endowments . . . came from Him, and are a trust for which we shall have to give account" (11). Even decades later, when there had been ample time for the Shakespeare sermon to become an established part of the Victorian religious and social calendar, the evident unease over the preaching of sermons on the life and works of a mortal man persisted. The Rev. G. F. Browne, in his Shakespeare sermon of 1893, for example, was so obviously unsympathetic to the endeavor that he preached nearly an entire sermon on the pernicious nature of secular literature, managing to avoid mention of Shakespeare at all until the very end, when he conceded only that "at worst no one can ever find in Shakespeare's plays an allurement to sin" (qtd. in Arbuthnot 20).

All in all the Shakespeare sermon as a Victorian institution hardly seems to fit the description of a coherent politico-moral program systematically imposed from above. But what, then, was the impetus for this consolidating culture of Shakespeare as religion? As we shall see, this question does not have a single answer, and if we return to our celebration texts, this time to Wordsworth's sermon, we may begin to get a sense of why this was so.

As I have already noted, Wordsworth's sermon, like Archbishop Trench's, relies on many of the arguments one might expect from a Victorian preacher. Developing the sentiment expressed in the text—"All thy works praise thee, O Lord . . . "—he distinguishes between the manner in which God is reflected in the beauty of the natural world and his reflection in the capacities of sentient human beings who reflect the Creator not merely passively, as do the trees and flowers, but through obedience of the reason and the will. Thus, we see in the works of Shakespeare, the national poet, the champion of right and good, the genius who was yet enough of a simple, sober-minded man to return to his native Stratford and there live out "his remaining days in rural quietude," the ultimate likeness:

> And as in the surface of that majestic stream the traveller sees a true reflection of the heavens which are above his head, so in the poetry of Shakespeare the reader may behold no uncertain image of the Word of God; may behold shining in its depths the starlike truths of the Bible; may behold and may adore the SUN OF RIGHTEOUSNESS, overclouded, we must confess, from time to time, with the mists of earth, but still shedding around His divine rays, and lighting up all with faith and hope, with love and joy. (Wordsworth, "Sermon" 404)

There are two issues that Wordsworth's sermon raises in the context of this discussion. The first, and most obvious, has to do with the problem of reflection and the extent to which it is tied to contemporary ideas about human genius and its relationship to divine inspiration. The second arises from Wordsworth's unmistakable caveat about "the mists of earth" overclouding the sun of righteousness. That Wordsworth's climactic passage should take up the question of the relationship between human genius and divine inspiration is not surprising, given the prevailing context of theological and literary debate. It was, after all, the 1860s and the turn to the German higher criticism, which provides a set of conditions in which the germinal culture of bardolatry could take root.

The influence of the German higher criticism in its radical reassessment of the status of the Bible had long been exercised on English intellectuals such as Samuel Taylor Coleridge, Thomas Carlyle, George Eliot, and George Henry Lewes. But when, in 1860, a group of radical clergymen followed suit by publishing a series of *Essays and Reviews* questioning elements of Anglican orthodoxy such as the predictive character of Old Testament prophecy, the possibility of miracles, and eternal damnation, the debate became a matter of public controversy. Perhaps most far-reaching in its effects was the claim advanced by Benjamin Jowett that "the Bible be read like any other book" (qtd. in Altholz 28). For, in signaling the fact that for many the Bible was ceasing to be a record of divine revelation and was becoming, instead, a work of literature, albeit one with an extraordinary provenance, Jowett was, by implication, signaling a corresponding alteration in the ways people thought about secular literature. While the radical impulses of the higher criticism may have been directed, in the first instance, at a reassessment of the status of the Bible, its effects in the sphere of secular literature were no less powerfully felt.

As a school of thought which married philosophical inquiry to detailed textual analysis, the higher criticism was uniquely well placed to bridge the traditional gap between sacred and secular texts. And what is interesting in terms of the effect of the higher criticism on attitudes toward secular literature is the way in which, despite its theological radicalism, it displaced rather than altogether dispensed with a sense of the divine. On the one hand, the higher criticism challenged the sacred status of the Bible by transforming it from a pure record of divine inspiration into a literary and mythological text that

could, and indeed ought to, be subject to scrutiny about its authorship, about the veracity of its historical claims, and about its formal
qualities. But, on the other, it retained the notion of inspiration, for,
though the "Old Testament prophets and the apostles of the New
were now to be considered as secular authors . . . were they not in
some sense [still] 'inspired' though not literally dictated by the Holy
Spirit?" (Shaffer 63).

Thus, two new and central questions were raised by the higher
criticism, one about the nature of "secular inspiration" (Shaffer 63),
the other about the character of the inspired author. And nowhere,
I would argue, were these questions more fully engaged than in
discourse about Shakespeare as the ultimate conduit of such inspiration and about his exalted texts. In short, the displacement of the
Bible as sacred text and literal word of God by a notion of the Bible
as literature always seemed to be offset, one way or another, by a
corresponding elevation of the status of secular literature—and,
iconically, the works of Shakespeare—from mere human expression,
however accomplished, to something semidivine. It was as if God
and Shakespeare occupied either end of a seesaw, the one falling
as the other rose, the relative position of each derived from the
energy of the other. And negotiating the transfer of belief from one
end of the seesaw to the other became a rather drawn-out affair, one
to which I will return.

To take up the second issue highlighted in Wordsworth's text—
namely, that of the mists of earth overclouding Shakespeare's brilliance, or, to put it in less poetic terms, the occurrence in Shakespeare's work of elements that were not obviously exemplary—this is
a question that had plagued admirers of Shakespeare for a long time.

Eighteenth-century discourse about Shakespeare's genius did not
necessarily assume a direct relation between it and the formal literary
or moral perfection of his work, a fact we can easily see if we look
at something like Samuel Johnson's "Preface to Shakespeare." For
when Johnson called Shakespeare the "poet of nature" he clearly did
not intend by this a comparison with something uncompromised in
its beauty and rational order. "The work of a correct and regular
writer," Johnson wrote:

> is a garden accurately formed and diligently planted . . .
> the composition of Shakespeare is a forest . . . inter-
> spersed sometimes with weeds and brambles . . . Other
> poets display cabinets of precious rarities minutely
> finished . . . [and] polished with brightness. Shakespeare
> opens a mine which contains gold and diamonds in inex-
> haustible plenty, though clouded by incrustations,
> debased by impurities, and mingled with a mass of
> meaner minerals. (34)

Thus, to say, within this context, that Shakespeare's plays are like
nature is to say that they are extraordinary, for better or for worse,
and that, as a body of work, therefore, they fail to display the refine-
ment and regularity one would expect from a text setting out an ethical code or moral plan. Rather, Shakespeare's morality is seen to be
haphazard. As Johnson put it, "precepts and axioms drop casually
from him," and his "examples . . . operate by chance" (21).

It was not until the intervention of Coleridge in the debate that
this view of Shakespeare as a *lusus naturae,* or sport of nature, and
of his plays as "works of rude uncultivated genius, in which the
splendour of the parts compensates . . . for the barbarous shapeless-
ness of the whole" (*Shakespearean Criticism* 1:197), was replaced by
a view of Shakespeare as the total genius and author of the most
perfect plays imaginable to humankind.[5] Coleridge maintained that
it was absurd to suppose that, on the one hand, Shakespeare was
a genius but that, on the other, his plays were sometimes terribly
flawed. This would mean that "here Shakespeare was below contempt; [while] there he rose above all praise. Here he displayed
an utter ignorance of human nature; there a most profound acquaintance with it" (2:76). "Shakespeare knew the human mind," Coleridge argued:

> and its most minute and intimate workings, and he
> never introduces a word, or a thought, in vain or out of
> place: if we do not understand him it is our own fault or
> the fault of copyists and typographers; but study, and
> the possession of some small stock of the knowledge by
> which he worked, will enable us often to detect and

> explain his meaning. He never wrote at random, or hit
> upon points of character by chance; and the smallest
> fragment of his mind not unfrequently gives a clue to a
> most perfect, regular, and consistent whole. (2:109)

As John Barrell points out, it is thus to this view of Coleridge's, above all, that we owe the situation that developed in the nineteenth century "that Shakespeare's plays are presumed to be so perfect . . . so entirely without fault, that if we find anything wrong with his plays, the fault must be with us and not with him" (n.p.). We find the profound influence of such a view in later, nineteenth-century ideas about Shakespeare and the Bible.

Insisting on the perfection of both the author and his works shifts the burden of responsibility onto the reader, for whom it becomes not just an intellectual but a moral duty to account *favorably* for everything in Shakespeare: the high and the low, the regular and the irregular, the exalted and the vulgar. And it is here, I would argue, in the assumptions manifested by this sense of obligation, that the Shakespearean text comes to approximate the status of the Bible— flawless, divinely authored, a book unlike all other books. Moreover, given that we are now dealing with an immaculate text, it follows that the practices of exegesis applied to it will need to display sufficient levels of intellectual rigor and moral commitment if its sacred mysteries are to be revealed. More than any other single influence, it is the logic of this belief which seems to drive the extraordinary production of writings about Shakespeare, religion, and the Bible from the 1860s onward, a body of writing to which I shall now turn.

II

Apart from the substantial collection of Shakespeare sermons which had accumulated by the turn of the century, writings on Shakespeare and the Bible or on Shakespeare and some other aspect of religion may be roughly divided into two types. First, there are writings about Shakespeare's own religious and moral affiliations. And, second, there are works that in some way advance the proposition that the complete works of Shakespeare do, indeed, constitute a secular equivalent to the Bible. Our main concern here will be with texts falling into this second category, but it will be helpful to say a little about the other first.

Works in the first category—namely, those seeking to prove, once and for all, that Shakespeare was either a Protestant or a Catholic—are remarkable mainly for their extreme petulance. Predictably, their arguments are, for the most part, based on spurious claims, highly selective readings of Shakespearean texts, and allegations of willful deception, forgery, and perversion often dragged out in serialized form in the scholarly press. While, admittedly, this has a certain amount of entertainment value for a late-twentieth-century reader, it is largely peripheral to a substantive understanding of late Victorian arguments about Shakespeare's relationship to the Bible, so I shall say no more about it here. Rather, I will concentrate on the category of texts which in some way advances the view that the relationship between the works of Shakespeare and the Bible was unique, the former becoming a secular version of the latter.

As I indicated earlier, the privileged relationship between Shakespeare and the Bible was fueled, in the first instance, by changing perceptions of the Bible's own status as a text. As James Bell put it in *Biblical and Shakespearian Characters Compared,* the Bible, although "no longer regarded by the majority of intelligent persons as a book of theological dogmas," has "superlative claims on literature" (5). Recognizing this, he maintained, "we can now do greater justice to the variety of the Bible than formerly—to its literary and dramatic and poetic qualities" (6). On the one hand, then, this process involved positively reinventing the Bible as literature. But, on the other hand, dispensing with the notion of divine authorship clearly also caused tremendous unease because it rendered ambiguous the status of the moral code to which many people had hitherto adhered. Hence, one finds arguments that seek to salvage the moral content of the Bible from the wreckage of divine authorship and, correspondingly, arguments in which the realm of secular literature, epitomized by the works of Shakespeare, becomes the net in which the moral and spiritual content of the Bible is gathered as it is pulled from this exploded notion of the Bible as the literal word of God. As Charles Bullock put it in *Shakspeare's Debt to the Bible:*

> In an age when "scientific jargon" and superficial
> speculation would fain persuade us that "our minds
> are moulded, and . . . our notions of duty are formed
> by the interaction of social forces," it is well to turn to
> the literary giants of the past, and learn from them that
> "the doctrine of religion, as well *moral* as mystical,
> depends upon Divine revelation." (5–6)

Great literature, in other words, would confirm belief, not interrogate or deny it. So moving the Bible from the realm of divinity into the realm of literature, should therefore not be read as a gesture of spiritual collapse so much as one of forced relocation.

A corollary to this line of argument (one we have already encountered in relation to the Shakespeare sermon) was used to negotiate the similarly fraught transition from revelation to literary accomplishment. For even outside the strictures of the homiletic form and the confines of the church, the divine origins of human genius was a persistent theme. "It is the prerogative of genius," wrote T. R. Eaton, in *Shakespeare and the Bible*, "to seem to create what it only receives and reproduces":

> Shakespeare went first to the word and then to the
> works of God. In shaping the truths derived from these
> sources he obeyed the highest instinct implanted by
> Him who had formed him *Shakespeare*. Hence his power
> of inspiring us with sublime affection for that which is
> properly good, and of chilling us with horror by his
> powerful delineations of evil. (12)

"But for the Bible," Charles Bullock maintained, "Shakespeare had been a Samson bereft of the power which constitutes the most important feature of his literary greatness" (56). "His writings are impregnated with the leaven of Revealed truth" (5).

Interestingly, even those writers who consciously refused the increasing tendency to conflate the word of Shakespeare and the word of God seem nevertheless unwittingly to have participated in reinforcing the association between the two. Charles Swinburne, in *Sacred and Shakespearian Affinities* (1890), for example, insisted that "there can be no actual comparison between the Book of Psalms and the writings of Shakespeare [because] the inspiration of the Psalmists . . . and the sacred subject matter of the Psalms would preclude it" (xxx–xxxi). Yet, despite his protestations of incomparability, and however purely philological his intentions, it is difficult to imagine a text that more perfectly inscribes the "Shakespeare as the Bible" mythology than the one he produced—namely, an imposing tome listing hundreds of pages of comparative usages in the manner of a concordance. Moreover, such intellectually and theologically reserved works were simply outnumbered, in the long run, by their rather more flamboyant and literal-minded counterparts. These may be typified by Charles Downing, who, in his volume *God in Shakespeare,* read the plays as a progressive revelation of Christian doctrine, and Charles Ellis who blithely reordered the sonnets and set each one facing a complementary passage from the Bible in order to reveal the mystical connections between the two. But, regardless of the approach, the effect of all this scholarship and speculation was clearly to reinforce, in both the popular and the scholarly mind, the belief that the Bible and the works of Shakespeare were somehow inextricably linked.

In this regard the Rev. Charles Plumptre, in a lecture entitled "The Religion and Morality of Shakespeare's Works," delivered before the Sunday Lecture Society in 1873, recounted the observations of two of his acquaintances. One, whom he described as "an intelligent woman . . . who, like most of us, had felt something of the . . . wisdom enshrined in the writings of the world's greatest poet," had been overheard in the following exclamation: "Next to the Bible," she declared, "I believe in Shakespeare." Furthermore, according to Plumptre, a "learned Professor," echoing this woman's sentiments, confirmed, albeit in a more scholarly manner, that Shakespeare's works have indeed "often been called a secular Bible." Therefore, he observed:

> Commonsense and erudition thus agree in recognising
> the same broad simplicity and universal natures . . . pre-
> served in these perennially popular books. Both alike
> deal with the greatest problems of Life; both open those

> questions which knock for answer at every human heart;
> both reflect the humanity which is common to us all.
> (10)

Other writers expressed comparable views. "A passage . . . rises in our thoughts, unaccompanied by a clear recollection of its origin. Our first impression," T. R. Eaton proposed, is "that it *must* belong *either* to the *Bible* or to *Shakespeare*" (12–13). In a somewhat more nationalistic spirit, James Bell gave voice to the popular belief that together "the English Bible and the Works of Shakespeare may fairly enough be called the two noblest possessions of the English-speaking peoples" (166). "They are the greatest achievements of the Anglo-Saxon race" (167), he declared, "twin inspirers of all that is best in life and thought, in aspiration and faith (178), reflecting "more real glory on our nation and our race, than the acquisition of India" (171). Back on the home front, Charles Wordsworth dedicated his study to his children, "in the hope . . . that they may grow up readers and lovers of Shakespeare as the Book of Man; But, still more, readers and lovers of the Bible as the word of God" (*Knowledge*).

Thus, despite occasional admonitions that the two texts were not, strictly speaking, comparable, since the works of Shakespeare were, after all, only metaphorically divine, the perceived affinities between them nevertheless fostered a widely held belief that Shakespeare's works did indeed constitute something like "a secular Bible" (Wordsworth, *Knowledge* 2), in effect, a body of writing which gave "a full and accurate system of religious doctrine" and from which one could therefore derive an ethical system or moral code (353). The situations represented in Shakespeare's plays were taken as an inventory of moral dilemmas, while his characters were seen to describe the complete range of possible responses to those dilemmas—in effect, the complete range of possibilities for human behavior. In this way Shakespeare's works became a source of moral authority second only, if indeed they were second, to the word of God or the Bible itself. "It is the spirit of love, of trust, of confidence in an all-wise and all merciful Creator," Plumptre said, "which is the Religion that Shakespeare preaches and inculcates" (11). "The solemn lesson which Shakespeare is so continually reinforcing," he argued, "is the sense of our responsibility to God and our accountability to him" (16). According to Plumptre, "the peculiarly Christian spirit . . . leavening the whole of Shakespeare's philosophy is everywhere observable" in his works (17–18), and thus, he urged us to conclude, "If there is any preacher who would deter us from sin and crime . . . it is Shakespeare" (14–15).

Here it will be worth underlining the fact that the Rev. Plumptre was far from unique in his opinions. Such testimonials commonly issued forth not just from impassioned laymen but from clergymen alike. Dr. Hugh McNeile, once dean of Ripon, claimed that "next to the Bible, I have derived more benefit from the study of Shakespeare than from any other human author" (qtd. in Wordsworth, *Knowledge* 357). Dr. John Sharpe, "one of the best and most esteemed prelates that ever sat upon the English bench," declared that "the Bible and Shakespeare have made me Archbishop of York" (ix). While a Rev. Chalmers looked upon Shakespeare as "nothing less than an intellectual miracle" (358).

At times these comparisons even threatened to extend themselves from the works in question to their respective authors. In one particularly ecstatic passage, for example, Plumptre declared:

> If force of genius . . . the heart of a man united to the imagination of a poet, and wielding the Briarean hands of a Demigod—if the promotion of the spirit of Charity and universal brotherhood; if these constitute for mortal man, titles to the name of Benefactor, and to that praise that ceases not with the sun but expands with immortality; then the name and the praise must support the throne which Shakespeare has established over the minds of the inhabitants of an earth which may be known in other parts of the Universe as Shakespeare's World. (24–25)

Admittedly, Plumptre's is a particularly baroque account of Shakespeare as religion, but the point to be made here is that, in other respects, his claims were not extraordinary at all. All thoughts of blasphemy seemed to vanish from people's minds when it came to the subject of Shakespeare and religion. Referring to Shakespeare,

Charles Ellis declared it "a treason to humanity to speak of such a one as in any sense a common place being" (*Shakspeare and the Bible* 9). Charles Downing barely had the words for it; for him "the profane play-actor was a Holy-Prophet—'Nay, I say unto you, and more than a Prophet,' the Messiah" (*God* 15).

We can see, then, the extraordinary weight of cultural authority which the Shakespearian text came to possess from the mid to late nineteenth century as a result of its unique association with that other, all-encompassing ethical code. What remains for us to explore are the even more extraordinary circumstances that gave *The Merchant of Venice* pride of place in that moral world.

2 Portia:
The White Woman's Burden

On 8 October 1887 the *Girl's Own Paper* invited its readers to participate in the first of a series of competitions involving "essay writing
on a great English author." On this inaugural occasion the magazine
solicited essays, of not more than six pages, on the subject "My
favourite heroine from Shakespeare." Advised to model their sub-
missions on an article by Mary Cowden Clarke entitled "Shakespeare
as the Girl's Friend," which had appeared in an earlier issue, prospective entrants were promised cash awards for the two best submis-
sions; first-, second-, and third-class certificates; and special voting
privileges in connection with the Girl's Own Order of Merit, a society formed to reward the accomplishments of girls and women
"who during the year have distinguished themselves most by either
their actions or their words" (*GOP* 8/10/87, 8).

The competition appears to have elicited an unprecedented response from the magazine's readership. As the editors reported, "the
competitors evidently . . . made their work a labour of love, the
result being that their papers show an amount of excellence far ex-
ceeding anything the examiners were prepared for." While in previous competitions, the editors said, "there have always been a few
very bad papers, quite worthless in every respect . . . no blots of this
kind have disfigured the present Competition" (*GOP* 10/3/88, 380).
Moreover, it is brought to our attention that, while the age of the
participants ranged from twelve to thirty-nine years, "more papers
[were] sent in by girls between twenty and thirty than . . . in any
previous competition" and "that . . . these entries were "perhaps the
best work . . . [ever] received in any of our competitions." Finally,
with regard to the choice of subjects, the editors noted that Shake-

spearean heroines "who successfully overcome their troubles have been six times more popular than those whose end is tragic" and that among these "Portia of Belmont has been long and away the most popular" with "more than a third of the papers . . . [being] devoted to her (381).

By all accounts, then, the competition would have to have been declared a success. But this being said, it was not altogether problem free; despite the general climate of approbation, there appeared to be one small blot disfiguring the competition after all. For a number of the entrants, we are told, "wandered from the subject in a curious manner" and marred their chances by "making their essays a vehicle for expressing their ideas on some social problem." More specifically, the editors lamented that "the vexed question of 'women's rights' was answerable for four of these failures" (*GOP* 10/3/88, 380).

While four out of dozens, if not hundreds, of entries would hardly seem to matter, in fact, these entries must have mattered a great deal, since they were singled out by the editors for public scrutiny. The first of the failed entries ran as follows:

> My favourite heroine from Shakespeare is the "Lady Lawyer, Portia." It is superfluous to describe her action and speeches in The Merchant of Venice. Far better will it be for me to transport her to the nineteenth century, and show how deeply she would have been interested in the great subject of women's rights . . . She is evidently Shakespeare's pet creation, and can we not deduce from this, that the great writer would give to women a more important position than they have hitherto occupied?

The second failed example, strikingly, takes precisely the opposite point of view:

> My heroine would not support any of those fanciful opinions, advocated by some women of the present day—opinions which, if carried out, would result in our clever girls becoming second-rate men instead of first-rate women.

The other two "failed" entries are not quoted but, we are told, line up similarly with one on either side of the divide, producing a situation in which diametrically opposed perspectives choose the same vehicle for promoting their position. Or, as the competition report has it, it was a "curious" situation in which "both those who approve of and those who disbelieve in what are known as 'Women's Rights' . . . choose the same heroine, Portia, and draw from her character directly opposite conclusions" (*GOP* 10/3/88, 381).

While an analysis of information as anecdotal as this must be necessarily speculative, the report does invoke a curious scenario. A series of essay-writing competitions on great English authors was initiated. The choice, both of Shakespeare as the first author and of favorite heroines as the first topic, seems self-evident enough. Far from self-evident, however, are the facts that the subject elicited responses from unprecedented numbers of women between the ages of twenty and thirty, that these entries were considered to be the most impressive received on any subject in any competition to date, and that the overwhelming identification of contestants was with triumphant rather than tragic heroines, and with Portia of Belmont most of all. Clearly, the high level of popular engagement with the subject suggests a convergence of issues of substantial importance to the participants, and discovering what those issues were and, more important, why they were being contested through the figure of Portia will be the primary aim of this chapter.

But while I take the apparent popularity of Portia as my starting point for this discussion, it is not in the many "worthy" entries but in what the editors deemed to be the few "unworthy" ones that the most arresting evidence of popular engagement with the figure of Portia can be found. For the unanticipated skirmish over "women's rights" and its very public censuring by the *Girl's Own Paper* editors alert us to a number of contentious issues lying beneath the surface of the competition. The four renegade contestants, in linking the tribulations of the Shakespearean heroine to trials of their own, clearly overstepped a boundary and expressed, in no uncertain terms, something that the other contestants could only imply through their collective identification with the figure of Portia and their shared enthusiasm for the project. The *Girl's Own Paper* was, admittedly, not the most obvious venue for political struggle and Portia of Belmont at best a darkhorse candidate for supreme icon of the contested status of women, but, if this anecdote tells us anything, I would argue, it is about the extent to which both these things were, precisely, the case.

In what follows my aim will be to identify some of the many issues that converged in the figure of Portia and explain why it was that, in the late nineteenth and early twentieth centuries she, above all, was the Shakespearean heroine everyone wanted to control. To begin, however, it will be helpful to establish a number of contextual issues in the ongoing history of women and Shakespeare.

I

Studying Shakespeare was supposed to be good for everyone, but it was thought to be especially good for women, and, conventionally, the benefits of studying Shakespeare were believed to be of four main types. First, studying Shakespeare was considered to be a virtue because it taught people about history and, in particular, about English history; second, it was considered valuable as an exercise in philology, since the texts display a wide range of linguistic forms; third, Shakespeare's works were said to constitute an unrivaled celebration of the English national character; and, fourth, because they were supposed to contain all of human experience, like the Bible, the *Collected Works of Shakespeare* were thought to provide a definitive guide for living. The first two reasons were widely quoted as benefiting students of Shakespeare at large, but the latter two were most laden with meaning when it came to women.

The first of these reasons—that Shakespeare embodied and conveyed Englishness in its highest form—took on special meanings with regard to women because, by invoking the putative links between cultural production and human reproduction, it added studying Shakespeare to the list of female occupations sanctioned by the discourse of civic maternalism and the eventual eugenic project of which it was a part. That middle-class English women at the time were being urged to commit their lives to breeding the fittest possible English subjects with the aim of sustaining the supremacy of the British Empire is a fact that has been extensively documented elsewhere.[1] With regard to women and Shakespeare the argument was, quite simply, that women who studied Shakespeare would be more English than women who did not. The more English that English women were, the better English mothers they would be, and better English mothers meant better English subjects to defend and maintain the empire. These arguments are by now well-known. Less familiar are those that proclaimed the ability of the Shakespearean text to provide a quasi-biblical guide for living, and these are crucial, for in the late nineteenth and early twentieth centuries this was the predominant form in which the special relationship between women and Shakespeare was played out.

While it was a Victorian commonplace to compare the works of Shakespeare to the Bible, the problem of disseminating the message of the Gospels remained. And of the various strategies employed toward this end the production of character typologies was among the most influential. Typologies could take the form of books (often issued in ornate editions) or parts of books that devoted each chapter or section to extolling the virtues of a particular heroine or group of heroines. Alternatively, typologies could take the shorter forms of essays (often serialized) or critical sketches that made ubiquitous appearances in periodicals as varied as the *Religio-Philosophical Journal* and the *Girl's Own Paper.* Typologies were a regular feature of school editions of Shakespeare which, in their notes for study and examination, invariably schematized the characters as socially representative types. And the influence of typologies was evident even in the memoirs of actresses such as Helena Faucit Martin and Ellen Terry, who structured autobiographical writings around experiences associated with their various Shakespearean roles.

Typologies classified and described characters from Shakespeare according to their moral and behavioral type and by this means sought to derive, from Shakespeare's dramatis personae, an orderly, comprehensive, and morally authoritative account of human, but especially female, nature. One early but enduringly influential example of such a typology may be found in Anna Jameson's *Characteristics of Women.*[2] In a chapter headed "Characters of Intellect" one finds the following passage:

> Portia, Isabella, Beatrice, and Rosalind, may be classed
> together, as characters of intellect, because, when com-
> pared with others, they are at once distinguished by their
> mental superiority. In Portia it is intellect, kindled into
> romance by a poetical imagination; in Isabel, it is intel-
> lect elevated by religious principle; in Beatrice, intellect
> animated by spirit; in Rosalind, intellect softened by sen-
> sibility. The wit which is lavished on each is profound,
> or pointed, or sparkling, or playful—but always femi-
> nine; like spirits distilled from flowers, it always reminds
> us of its origin;—it is a volatile essence, sweet as power-
> ful; and to pursue the comparison a step further, the wit
> of Portia is like attar of roses, rich and concentrated; that
> of Rosalind, like cotton dipped in aromatic vinegar; the
> wit of Beatrice is like sal volatile; and that of Isabel, like
> the incense wafted to heaven . . . it is difficult to pro-
> nounce which is most perfect in its way . . . But . . . I
> believe we must assign the first rank to Portia, as uniting
> in herself in a more eminent degree than the others, all
> the noblest and most loveable qualities that ever met
> together in woman. (5)

Throughout the nineteenth century, but overwhelmingly during the
1880s and 1890s, deriving such essential moral schemes from Shakespeare was an extremely popular thing to do. In fact, the practice was
so widespread that it would be impossible even to guess at the number of typologies produced; to talk about Shakespeare at the time
was, largely, to classify and evaluate his characters as moral types.

Typologies could function in a number of ways. Most explicitly,
they invited you to identify with a heroine of your choice and then
be like her or, as we shall see in the case of someone like Lady Macbeth, not be like her. But typologies also operated in more complex
ways and at other levels. If Shakespeare was the world, then typologies were maps of that world; they were the representational form
that allowed you to gain your moral orientation and thus tackle any
experience the world was apt to offer up. As Mary Cowden Clarke
argued in her essay "Shakespeare as the Girl's Friend":

> To the young girl, emerging from childhood and taking
> her first step into the more active and self-dependent
> career of woman-life, Shakespeare's vital precepts and
> models render him essentially a helping friend. To her he
> comes instructively and aidingly; in his pages she may
> find warming guidance, kindliest monition, and wisest
> council. Through his feminine portraits she may see, as
> in a faithful glass, pictures of what she has to evitate, or
> what she has to imitate, in order to become a worthy
> and admirable woman. (562)

Each of Shakespeare's one hundred and twenty-six female characters
was seen as having a vital lesson to offer. In the figure of Desde-
mona, for example, Mary Cowden Clarke found that "Shakespeare
has read all gentle-charactered women a lesson" on the "grave error
of a clandestine and runaway marriage," while "in Helena we have a
vigorous example of moral courage, perseverance, and steadfast faith
in the power of self-help, together with a womanly self-abnegation
and self-diffidence, when comparing herself and the man she loves"
(563). In sum, typologies made it easier to turn to Shakespeare as a
guide for living and, it should be noted, as they accumulated in the
thousands, made him progressively harder to ignore.

In other cases typologies were taken up, more casually, like mail-
order catalogs of humankind which a reader could browse through
at leisure, selecting models of heroism and virtue to emulate while
simultaneously learning to eschew villainy, all from the safety and
comfort of home. Admittedly, from the distance of a century or more
Shakespearean typologies have come to seem quaint, if not absurd.
Yet, though such characterizations are apt enough, they should not
be allowed to obscure the extent to which typologies of female characters from Shakespeare were effective in limiting the range of acceptable behaviors for women at a time when the restrictions on female
social mobility were being seriously challenged.

In order to get a sense of how the typological construct of "Shakespeare's women" was used to censure the behavior of real women
living in the world outside his plays, I would like to consider an article entitled "On the Study of Shakespeare for Girls," written by a

woman named Kathleen Knox (otherwise known as a writer of didactic children's fiction) which appeared in the *Journal of Education* in April 1895.

At the outset something must be said about the status of Mrs. Knox's text. For, while the piece takes the form of an open letter in reply to correspondence allegedly sent to the author by a girl named Dorothy, for several reasons this fact seems more apparent than real. Specifically, the *Journal of Education* is an unlikely thing for a young girl to have been reading; Dorothy's letter is always conspicuously paraphrased rather than quoted; and, if Mrs. Knox's account of the child's letter is to be believed, she managed, in the course of her inquiry, to raise virtually every major question about Shakespeare study in relation to the middle-class female population in contemporary pedagogical debate. These things in combination suggest that the letter was, frankly, contrived in order to address what must have been a familiar classroom scenario and to provide guidelines for teachers who were themselves regularly faced with the sorts of questions Dorothy supposedly asked.

"My Dear Dorothy" the letter begins:

> There was no need to apologise for your long letter, nor even for its untidiness; so deep was my interest in its contents, that I quite disregarded the blots which my impetuous young friend plentifully scattered over the pages in her excitement. And all about the study of Shakespeare for girls, one of the most interesting subjects which could be proposed to me for consideration, and which, indeed, is very often in my mind.

From here the author goes on to summarize the complaints that Dorothy lodges against Shakespeare as follows: that the systematic study of Shakespeare such as one has to undertake in order to pass a Cambridge local examination is "dry, difficult, and uninteresting"; that plays that were clearly meant to provide entertainment for a previous age provided nothing but "pain and grief" in the present era; and that it was, at best, unclear what there was in Shakespeare that made people "rave" about him as they did. In sum, it was unclear to Dorothy "why one should 'learn' Shakespeare at all" (222). In reply to these concerns Kathleen Knox offered the following analysis.

"You ask," Mrs. Knox began, why "what was pleasure in one generation should be pain in another [and you say that] people are different now," that "tastes have changed." "My dear girl," Mrs. Knox replied, "*tastes* will change, [but] human instincts never":

> Human instinct can no more get tired of love, mirth, pity, terror, and death as presented to them by a great artist, than they can get tired of the sun. People and tastes are very different now, but in one thing they remain the same, in love of Shakespeare.

The real difference, according to Mrs. Knox, "lies not in the number of those who love him, but in the number of those who can read." And, though it might seem to us that a higher rate of literacy would see the value of Shakespeare's stock rise, in fact, Kathleen Knox was arguing precisely the opposite. The problem, as she saw it, was not that people don't love Shakespeare anymore because they can't read but, rather, that they don't love him the way they used to because they *can* read and, unfortunately, are too busy reading other things (222).

Yet, while Mrs. Knox declared this to be a "bad state of affairs," she was willing to concede that Dorothy was not entirely at fault. "We are all more or less slaves to the age in which we live," she wrote, "and you have been born in an age in which . . . schoolgirls . . . are allowed to indulge in indiscriminate reading." Contrary to current presumption, Mrs. Knox maintained that "a bright and active mind, a profound interest in all the everyday concerns of life, [and] an extensive acquaintance with all the lighter papers, magazines, and novels of the day" would not stand a young lady in good stead. Rather, these things may tend to make her contemptuous of anything that "does not square with . . . [her] own experience, or could not happen in an age of bicycles and telephones." "The best kind of literature," Mrs. Knox declared, "has no affinity with bicycles and telephones!" (222).

Yet, despite this gloomy outlook, all was not lost. There was yet a way in which Dorothy and other girls like her could redeem their relationships to Shakespeare, and, according to Kathleen Knox, it was this:

> Some sunshiny spring or summer Saturday, go out into
> . . . the woods, ask your best . . . friend to go with you,
> and take a volume of Shakespeare [along]. Do not take
> the school edition, but the daintiest and prettiest volume
> you can find . . . and lay in it a sprig of scented geranium
> . . . to mark the place and be a pleasure to the senses.
> Sternly resist the temptation . . . to spend the time lying
> under a tree, talking school gossip, or reading the last
> number of "Martin Hewitt, Investigator" . . . and read
> the play through with your friend . . . The next Shake-
> speare day in class, I think, some breath of the summer
> wood and the scent of the geranium will blow on your
> Clarendon Press edition, and you and your friend will
> exchange a sly smile of superior intelligence! Do this,
> not once, but many times, and . . . the temptation to
> take out "an amusing book" [will] become less and less
> . . . [Y]ou will learn to understand the beauty of the
> poetry as well as the story of Shakespeare's plays. All the
> human wisdom that is to be found in them you cannot
> know till later. (223–23)

This wisdom, Mrs. Knox explained, is somehow buried in Shakespeare, invisible and unarticulated. But, though, she told Dorothy, it
is something you may not understand now:

> You can imbibe it unconsciously to bear fruit in the
> woman's life you will have to lead hereafter. And in this
> age of feminine eagerness and prominence, when every-
> thing in life, literature, and science is being attempted by
> women, and often . . . with woeful lack of judgment, it
> will be well to have such a standard of sanity, modera-
> tion, and harmony as is presented to us by Shakespeare's
> world . . . Among all literary artists Shakespeare stands
> pre-eminent in the creation of lovely women—lovely in
> body and soul . . . Study Shakespeare's women, and be
> assured that without the[m] all the enlightenment and
> freedom of the nineteenth century will but serve to make

you a byword in your generation. Resolve, while yet in
your teens to be a Shakespeare woman. (223)

This episode raises a number of questions. For instance, how are
we to understand Mrs. Knox's perception of an inverse relation between the level of literacy and the general level of culture? What are
we to make of her suggestion that a sort of Shakespearean Teddy
Bear's Picnic will somehow redress the ills of industrial society? And
what, exactly, is a "Shakespeare woman"?

Unquestionably, what Mrs. Knox was responding to was one version of the crisis of modernity as it was played out in relation to the
English, female middle class. In this scenario young ladies riding bicycles, talking on the telephone, and, most important, reading what
they like become signifiers of radical disorder and of irreversible
change. Sending them off to read Shakespeare in the woods—where
the conspicuous presence of nature will help restore a sense of the
true order of things—was an attempt to move young ladies away
from the menace and disorder of the modern city and from the innumerable forms of corruption to which they might be exposed. Kathleen Knox's vision of young ladies in the woods reading Shakespeare
expresses a yearning for a return to Eden, where one might dare to
hope that there, in that garden, away from bicycles and telephones,
young ladies might live purely, imbibe the spirit of Shakespeare, and
emerge as immaculate and fully fledged Shakespeare women. And it
is to this extraordinary persona that we now must turn.

I I

Without a doubt the best example of a Shakespeare woman is supplied by the figure of Mary Cowden Clarke. Née Mary Victoria
Novello (1809–98), Mary Cowden Clarke was raised in a distinguished literary family that moved in the same circles as Leigh Hunt
and Charles and Mary Lamb. She knew John Keats and Percy and
Mary Shelley as frequent visitors to her parents' home and later in life
became an acquaintance of Charles Dickens. While it wasn't until
after her marriage to Charles Cowden Clarke in 1828 that the extent
of Mary's involvement with Shakespeare became evident, her passage

through life was structured at every stage by her developing relation to the bard:

> Reared on Shakespeare . . . from the Lamb's Tales she
> . . . progressed to the plays themselves, and under the
> guidance of such mentors as [Leigh] Hunt and her hus-
> band-to-be . . . had become a confirmed Shakespearean,
> so far as that connotes abandonate sentimental passion
> for "England's brightest ornament." (Altick, *Cowden
> Clarkes* 116–17)

Mary herself endorsed this view in her essay "Shakespeare as the Girl's Friend," in which she advocated a modus vivendi evidently based on rewarding personal experience. "Happy is she," Mary Cowden Clarke wrote, "who at eight or nine . . . has a copy of Lamb's Tales from Shakespeare given to her":

> Happy she who at twelve or thirteen has Shakespeare's
> works themselves read to her by her mother, with loving
> selection of fittest plays and passages . . . Happy they
> who in maturer years have the good taste and good
> sense to read aright the pages of Shakespeare, and gather
> thence the wholesomest lessons and choicest delights!
> (564)

The Cowden Clarkes were considered to be one of the great liter-ary couples of all time. Their biographer claims that Charles and Mary "were extremely conscious of the fact that their marriage was the happiest one in all the kingdom" and that "among the literary couples of the age, not even the Brownings felt a tithe of the inno-cent ecstasy which permeated every waking hour of the Cowden Clarkes' unending honeymoon" (Altick, *Cowden Clarkes* 81). This is an extraordinary claim, and one would be hard pressed to contest it, but it may at least be fair to suggest that the Cowden Clarkes' un-ending honeymoon was actually more of a chronic ménage à trois. For, as Charles and Mary played out their marriage of true minds, it was Shakespeare who determined the shape of their lives.

The Cowden Clarkes' home was a virtual Shakespeare shrine. In their garden was "a monumental bust of the poet; in the hall, a copy of the Stratford monument . . . on Mary's finger, a signet ring of Shakespeare's head with which she sealed all her letters," and over her bed an image of "Angel William" so that it was "the first face— together with my mother's . . . to greet my waking eyes" (qtd. in Altick, *Cowden Clarkes* 126). The actual work that absorbed the Cowden Clarkes' energies was varied. Charles gained notoriety for the many articles he published on Shakespeare and for the lectures he delivered both at working men's colleges and on the public lecture circuit. The truly remarkable efforts, however, belonged to Mary. Like Charles, she also produced numerous short studies and articles mainly on characters in Shakespeare but also two long and rather extraordinary works. The first of these is a set of fifteen novellas collectively entitled *The Girlhood of Shakespeare's Heroines* (to which I will return) and the second her *Complete Concordance to Shakespeare.*

Apparently in response to the conversational remark that, "although there was a concordance to the Bible, no complete guide existed to 'the Bible of the Intellectual World,' Shakespeare's plays" (Altick, *Cowden Clarkes* 116), Mary Cowden Clarke, on a whim, undertook a project that was to consume the next sixteen years of her life. In what might well be described as the ultimate act of Victorian household management, she produced a concordance to the works of Shakespeare constituting some 309,600 entries. She worked from four to six hours a day transcribing, cross-referencing, and collating entries on small slips of paper, with twelve years of compilation followed by four years of proofreading text, delivered at 360 entries to a quarto page (122). Despite what must have been the incalculable personal cost of such an undertaking her biographer insisted that "there is no record of her ever having become discouraged." Rather, working alongside her husband while he prepared his public lectures on Shakespeare, Mary Cowden Clarke is said to have found in her private epic a source of "supreme happiness" (118).

The products of Mary Cowden Clarke's labor were monumental in more than one regard but, ironically, were perhaps most effective where they were least intended. For, while the *Concordance* was widely consulted until 1894, when it was superseded by a new concordance by Bartlett, its usefulness was seriously limited by the omission of line numbers, an omission that Mary Cowden Clarke had naively hoped would enhance the universality of the *Concordance* by making it "equally useful with all editions of Shakespeare." By way of contrast, however, the project's resonance in other spheres was undiminished, even after its textual authority had been overruled. For in addition to being a map of the world that was Shakespeare, Mary Cowden Clarke's *Concordance* marked the boundaries of the public/private divide, by standing as "a monument of feminine tenacity, of resolute, unquestioning devotion to a self-chosen labour" (Altick, *Cowden Clarkes* 122). While the project was conceived to provide what Mary Cowden Clarke believed had "long been a desideratum in all Libraries" (120), it served equally to valorize the sexual division of labor and the harnessing of female organizational talent to facilitate the scholarly pursuits of men. As one of her admirers described it, the *Concordance* was "a votive lamp lighted at the shrine of the poet" (qtd. in Altick, *Cowden Clarkes* 124).

The virtues that Mary Cowden Clarke exemplified through her work on the *Concordance* found parallel expression in her writings on characters—especially female characters—in Shakespeare. And her most imposing work in this genre is, without a doubt, *The Girlhood of Shakespeare's Heroines*. In this work, employing a clear if somewhat skewed typological principle, she sought to explain the behavior of female characters in Shakespeare by writing retroactive accounts of their lives up until the moment at which the play begins. Here it may be helpful briefly to clarify why such a gesture might be necessary.

If Shakespeare was the total universal genius, which he was for a nineteenth-century audience, as I argued in chapter 1, it then necessarily follows that both the characters and the situations he represented must always be exemplary. But, while this assumption was what allowed people to say: "Portia is an exemplary female. Try to be more like Portia," it was also what caused such people to shoot themselves in the foot with regard to female characters who, for example, dress up in men's clothing, refuse to marry, and occasionally kill people. Various critical and pedagogical strategies were employed to deal with this inconvenience, and what I am suggesting with regard to *The Girlhood of Shakespeare's Heroines* is that these retroactively apologetic texts were Mary Cowden Clarke's contribution to this pool of strategic wisdom. An illustration will serve to demonstrate how this works.

Lady Macbeth, it hardly needs pointing out, does not easily accommodate the "Angel in the House" model of Victorian bourgeois domesticity. In what sense, then, could she be considered to set a standard of "sanity, moderation, and harmony," to recall Mrs Knox's formulation? Not surprisingly, it was by negative example that she did so. According to Mary Cowden Clarke, in her novella *The Thane's Daughter,* the difficulties with Lady Macbeth's character are attributable to a complex series of misfortunes. Her mother longs for a son and is so bitterly disappointed at the birth of a daughter that she curses the child, refuses to show her appropriate motherly attention, and eventually dies as a result of her own disappointment. Left in the care of her weak, unmasculine father, there is nothing to prevent Lady Macbeth from running around the castle as she likes and growing up wild. One day she stumbles upon the room in which they keep the armor, unleashes a secret passion for combat, and the rest, as they say, is history. Although any one of these unfortunate circumstances would probably have been considered enough to ruin a daughter, Mary Cowden Clarke takes no chances, rolling them all up into one. Take an unmotherly mother, an unfatherly father, and a lack of adequate supervision, and what do you get? Lady Macbeth. The tale was a cautionary one for a Victorian audience, destined, in Mary Cowden Clarke's words, "to be read [as] a world-wide lesson, how unhallowed desires and towering ambition can deface the image of virtue in a human heart and teach it to spurn and outrage the dictates of nature itself." Here we might want to invoke Mrs. Knox's warning about the woeful lack of judgment which, in her view, attended the age of feminine eagerness and prominence. For nineteenth-century opponents of feminism there would have been more than a figurative relation between the persona of the New Woman and the character of Lady Macbeth.

The Thane's Daughter gives us an idea of how these texts operate generally, but to return to our own heroine it should be noted that the series was, in fact, inspired by the figure of Portia. Hazlitt, in *Characters from Shakespeare's Plays,* had disparaged Portia as a woman

displaying a "certain degree of affectation and pedantry" (qtd. in Altick, *Cowden Clarkes* 138). Apparently anxious to defend "a favourite
character," Mary Cowden Clarke rose to the occasion by providing an
extended apologia for Portia's nature in the form of a novella entitled
Portia: The Heiress of Belmont.

In Mary Cowden Clarke's novella the Portia of Shakespeare's drama
is reckoned to be the child of a certain Guido di Belmonte and Portia, sister of Bellario. After the untimely death of the latter, Guido,
stricken with grief, goes into seclusion, giving over the infant Portia
to the care of her uncle. It is thus the child's upbringing by the lawyer
Bellario which constitutes much of the matter of the novella and an-
ticipates Portia's appearance in the courtroom in Shakespeare's play.
Imbued with a passion for learning, Portia loves nothing better than
to listen to Bellario discourse on the law. And, not surprisingly,
Mary Cowden Clarke composed these speeches with Shakespeare's
drama in mind so that, for example, she anticipated the "quality of
mercy" speech with a long passage on the divine origins of the law
and the spuriousness of Shylock's legal claim with explicit warnings
from Bellario that, "by taking the law in our own hands, we but per-
petuate evil in the world; dealing a private revenge, instead of award-
ing a publicly sanctioned punishment" (*Girlhood* 41–42).

Most notable is a passage on the practice of the law in which Mary
Cowden Clarke was clearly responding to Hazlitt's view of Portia as
an affected and unwomanly pedant. Here what has been dominantly
represented as the public and paternalistic nature of the law admits
the influence of "Mercy . . . fairest sister of Justice" (*Girlhood* 42–43).
"The practice of Law," says Bellario,

> teaches us tolerance towards the infirmities of our
> fellow-beings . . . it engenders compassion for human
> frailty . . . pity for his imperfections, and desire for his
> enlightenment. It inculcates benevolence, patience and
> consideration. It bids us grieve over the evil we discover,
> and wonder at the good we find hidden beneath rags,
> neglect, and destitution . . . We should cultivate a
> patient and attentive habit of listening, acuteness of
> penetration in observing, and an appreciation of
> physiognomy, expression, and character. (43)

The fact that the description Bellario offers so obviously evokes many of the attributes of Victorian femininity—patience, compassion, charity, and benevolence, for example—does not escape the young Portia. "Might not we women make good advocates then?" she asks. But, anticipating complaints about Portia's careerist tendencies, Mary Cowden Clarke carefully reinscribed the bounds of woman's nature:

> It is because your hearts generally take too active a part
> in any cause you desire to win that your sex would make
> but poor lawyers . . . women though shrewd and quick
> judging are apt to jump too rapidly at conclusions and
> mar the power of their understanding . . . To skilfully
> treasure up each point successively gained, and by a
> tardy unmasking of your own plan of action, to lead
> your opponent on to other and more sure committals of
> himself, is more consonant with the operation of a man's
> mind, than suited to the eager, impulsive nature of
> woman. Her wit is more keen, than her understanding is
> sedate. (43–44)

The feminine virtues of mercy are of value only insofar as they temper and complement the operation of masculine justice. Through their comprehensive intuition of human needs they facilitate the actions of men by providing a concordance to the social environment. The delight with which Bellario tutors Portia in the law and with which Charles Cowden Clarke initiated his young wife into the mysteries of Shakespeare is strictly private. Women may study the law but only in order that they may more effectively discharge their domestic duties. As Mary Cowden Clarke had Bellario argue: "My Portia will become quite as proficient as I could wish her, if she know enough of law to manage . . . her own estate" (*Girlhood* 44).

Yet, despite the peerless example set, both in life and in writing, by Mary Cowden Clarke, the program for Shakespeare womanhood devised by Kathleen Knox, and the sheer profusion of Shakespeare typologies, Dorothy and the girls from the *Girl's Own Paper* competition somehow got it wrong and identified Portia as a site of struggle rather than one of exemplary feminine acquiescence. It is, there-

fore, to this struggle over the figure of Portia, the most highly prized
of all Shakespeare women, that we must now direct our attention.

I I I

Today it is probably impossible to think of Portia as anyone other
than that woman in *The Merchant of Venice* who dresses up as a lawyer, speaks movingly on the quality of mercy, and saves the merchant
Antonio from the evil Jew, Shylock. A hundred years ago it is more
than likely that Portia's participation in Antonio's trial would have
come only secondarily to mind, for the most striking feature of late
Victorian and early-twentieth-century discourse about Portia in relation to *The Merchant of Venice* is that her appearance in the trial scene
was of marginal importance to the play. Despite the fact that it is in
the trial scene that the typological imperative is fulfilled as Portia's
New Testament eloquence defeats Shylock's Old Testament justice
and, furthermore, that logic would militate against locating the cli-
max of a five act drama early in act 3, this is precisely what vast numbers of readers, viewers, and interpreters of *The Merchant of Venice*
did. Virtually without exception, it was not Portia's proverbial appeal
to "the quality of mercy" but her betrothal speech to Bassanio which
conveyed a sense of the heroine's exemplary femininity. In short, to
a late Victorian audience the Portia who was the paragon of the
Shakespeare woman was not the woman in the courtroom but,
rather, the woman who held her breath while her true love chose the
appropriate casket and the woman who then declared:

> You see me, Lord Bassanio, where I stand,
> Such as I am. Though for myself alone
> I would not be ambitious in my wish
> To wish myself much better, yet for you
> I would be trebled twenty times myself,
> A thousand times more fair, ten thousand times
> More rich, that only to stand high in your account,
> I might in virtues, beauties, livings, friends,
> Exceed account; but the full sum of me
> Is sum of something, which to term in gross,
> Is an unlessoned girl, unschooled, unpractised,
> Happy in this, she is not so old

> But she may learn; happier than this,
> She is not bred so dull but she can learn;
> Happiest of all is that her gentle spirit
> Commits itself to yours to be directed,
> As from her lord, her governor, her king.
> Myself and what is mine to you and yours
> Is now converted. But now I was the lord
> Of this fair mansion, master of my servants,
> Queen o'er myself; and even now, but now,
> This house, these servants, and this same myself
> Are yours . . .
>
> (III.ii.149–71)

The popular importance this moment in the play held, in contrast with Portia's appearance in the courtroom, can be gauged by a number of examples.

Mary Cowden Clarke's catalog of female virtue, "Shakespeare as the Girl's Friend," makes no mention whatsoever of Portia's participation in Antonio's trial. For her the heroine's virtue was expressed exclusively through

> the sweet dignity, combined with simplest modesty, con-
> spicuous in Portia of Belmont's acceptance of Bassanio,
> when he has won her according to her father's will by
> choice of the right casket. It is the born lady who
> speaks—ladylike in her accustomed graciousness and
> dignified bearing—ladylike in its simplicity, modesty,
> and generous humility. (563)

Similarly, for Helena Faucit Martin what is memorable when we leave our heroine, is the fact that we leave her

> in the gratified joy of having given to her husband not
> only "her house, her servants, and herself," but of having
> also, by her fine intelligence, rescued and restored him to
> his best friend and kinsman. (26)

A comparable, though visibly more tortured, view was posited by Mrs. M. L. Elliott in her work *Shakespeare's Garden of Girls*. While she was compelled to describe Portia as "Shakespeare's type of a strong-minded woman," Mrs. Elliott was eager to dispel any association between the Shakespearean type and contemporary manifestations of female independence. "How different," she argued, "is [Shakespeare's] idea from the popular one current at the present day":

> Portia is no hard-featured, loud talking, forbidding-looking being in semi-masculine or dowdy attire, but one endowed with all a Juliet's passion, and radiant with a consuming fire. She is indeed polished and sagacious, gifted and well-balanced, distinguished for intellectual excellence and superior common-sense, but she is none the less subject to the overmastering power of the affections. (117)

"Immeasurably superior as . . . [Portia] is to Bassanio," Mrs. Elliott wrote, "she would scorn the very idea of his inferiority. He is . . . as a god unto her, and upon his altar she would pour forth her whole soul" (118). "What to Portia were servants, lands, and livings in the presence of this new-found happiness?" she asked.

> Women glory in the complete divestment of all but love, not perhaps in this mercenary age, when they sell themselves for titles, gold, and position, but wherever nature is uncorrupted by greed, and the heart is unwarped from its innate instincts of rectitude. (119)

Ellen Terry, in her account of the first time she ever played Portia (Bancroft's production in 1875), linked her success to the very same aspect of the role:

> I had had some success in other parts, and had tasted the delight of knowing that audiences liked me . . . But never until I appeared as Portia . . . had I experienced that awe-struck feeling which comes . . . to no actress more than once in a life-time—the feeling of the conqueror . . . I knew that I had "got them" at the moment when I spoke the speech beginning, "You see me, Lord Bassanio, where I stand." (*Memoirs* 86)

On those infrequent occasions when commentators have made reference to the trial scene, Portia's participation in it has been carefully wrapped in the same quasi-religious discourse of self-denial. Typical of this approach is Henry Kelsey White, in his study of "Woman in Shakespeare":

> Was it not in the service of her husband's dearest friend that Portia donned the doctor's robe, and on his behalf that she spoke the noble lines on mercy? . . . Yes, it was in this attitude of sacred service . . . that Shakespeare seemed to delight to place the women of his thought, and thus were they enabled to display those transcendent and victorious virtues of self-sacrifice and self-surrender which are assuredly the most essential elements of the love that is most divine. (25)

Clearly, then, the moment was a key one in the play, but what was it, more precisely, about Portia's betrothal speech to Bassanio which consistently elicited such impassioned responses? And why, in light of its relative neglect today, were people then so riveted to act 3, scene 2, of *The Merchant of Venice*?

For a late-nineteenth- and early-twentieth-century audience Portia's betrothal speech to Bassanio was the most important part of the play, at least as far as Portia was concerned, because it provided a rejoinder to the manifesto of the New Woman. Portia had it all—ambition, independence, education, wealth, property—yet somehow she retained the traditional feminine attributes of selflessness, obedience, and virtue which the New Woman had cast aside. Her ambition was not for herself but for Bassanio, and her riches were of value only insofar as they were valued by him. Despite all her independence and accomplishments Portia was still, by her own account, an "unlessoned girl" eager to be "directed/As from her lord, her governor, her king," and willing to relinquish without hesitation her house, her servants, and indeed herself. In short, here was a woman who had it all and was, nevertheless, willing to give it up once she had found the right man. Or at least this was how it seemed to those who persistently located act 3, scene 2, as the moral center of the play.

While this reading was tremendously widespread and highly in-fluential, however, it always seemed to carry within it the seeds of its own undoing. For the surety with which people pointed to the be-trothal speech was more than matched by the anxieties they betrayed about other aspects of the text.

One such set of anxieties centered on matters of womanly virtue, since Portia, as an unmarried orphaned female, had no one and noth-ing, apart from the legacy of the three caskets, to regulate her amo-rous behavior. Anxieties about Portia's sexuality converged around a number of issues but, intriguingly, were particularly evident in responses to Ellen Terry's portrayal of the character in Irving's Ly-ceum production of *The Merchant,* undoubtedly compounded by the precedents for unorthodox behavior which the actress had set throughout her own life. Married and divorced for the first of three times while still in her teens, as well as being the lover of the architect Edwin Godwin and the mother of his two illegitimate children, Terry would have been as notable for her disregard of social conven-tion as she would have been for her work as an actress at that time. Her portrayal of Portia is reputed to have embodied many of the unconventional attitudes she held toward relations between men and women.

Richard Foulkes has pointed out that Portia's "father's will was not allowed to loom oppressively large" (Foulkes, "Helen Faucit" 29) in the production and suggests:

> one cannot help thinking that, if her father's absurd
> legacy of the caskets had resulted in the choice of an
> uncongenial husband, Portia would not have found it
> difficult to set aside the parental injunction in spirit if
> not in letter. At any rate we may safely prophecy that an
> unacceptable husband would not have had it all his own
> way. (Marshall, qtd. in Foulkes, "Helen Faucit" 29)

Terry herself had made the very same point about Portia, Beatrice, and Rosalind, when she declared, in a lecture entitled "The Tri-umphant Women," that "had they been disappointed in love they would have . . . [simply] set about making another life" (qtd. in Foulkes, "Helen Faucit" 29). Moreover, Terry's interpretation of the role made no effort to conceal Portia's physical interest in the man whom she desires but who has not yet become her wedded husband. This display led Henry James to complain that Terry's Portia was altogether too "osculatory in her relations to Bassanio" (qtd. in Manvell 130) and Ruskin to protest that "the speech, 'You see me Lord Bassanio . . .' would . . . produce its true effect on the audience only if spoken with at least half a dozen yards" between the two characters (131–32). In a similar vein *Blackwood's Magazine* accused the actress of "indelicacy" for "holding Bassanio 'caressingly by the hand, almost in an embrace' when she urged him to tarry awhile before choosing" (Hughes 235). Yet Terry's Portia apparently had quite a different effect on the male population at large, prompting "a flood of letters from men expressing their admiration for her." "Everyone," she remarked, "seemed to be in love with me!" (qtd. in Manvell 95).

But Portia didn't need Ellen Terry to make her complicated; that was something the character could manage very well on her own. For the idea of a wealthy, unmarried, orphaned female would have been fantastically attractive to the rather less unrestricted young women of the day, and concern over the precedent that identification with such a figure might set is, accordingly, evident in popular discourse about two further issues associated with Portia's virtue— namely, those of obedience to the absent father and of generosity toward the indigent husband.

The question of Portia's obedience to her absent father arises, naturally enough, in relation to the legacy of the three caskets. Here commentators were at pains to construct the issue as one of filial piety by emphasizing the fact that Portia is "faithful to her father's dying wishes . . . although these seemed to put her future happiness at the mercy of chance" (Crook liv). While it may be admitted that "in a moment of depression Portia once fretted against the restraint imposed on her by her father's will," we are assured that "she afterwards expressed her real intention," namely, to "'die as chaste as Diana, unless I be obtained by the manner of my father's will'" (Wood, Supplement 13). Remarkably, no real effort was made to disguise the less elevated sentiments that, in practice, constituted the notion of filial piety. The identification of women as a site of struggle between fathers and potential husbands and the need for maintaining women in a state of dependence are unapologetically evident in this passage from Stanley Wood's Dinglewood Shakespeare Manuals:

> Portia, an orphan, young, and endowed with almost fabulous wealth, would have been exposed to many dangers in her completely isolated position. Her father's will was calculated not only to secure her from the intrigues of unprincipled adventurers, but also to keep her in a state of dependence and subordination appropriate to the female sex. She herself was fully aware of the wisdom and kindness of her father's command. (8)

A similar interest in women's selfless generosity dominated discourse about Portia's largesse with regard to Bassanio and her part in the attempt to save Antonio's life. Here, exploiting a strange sort of "what's mine is yours; what's yours is mine" logic, commentators argued that it is only fair that Portia should share her wealth with Bassanio, since he has freely offered to share his problems with her. We are told, for example, that, on learning of the threat to Antonio's life, Portia

> demands as a right her share in the sorrow he [Bassanio] has to bear . . . hurries off Bassanio with ducats sufficient to pay the bond twelve times over . . . and determines to take a part herself in the effort for Antonio's release. (Crook liv–lv)

Or, as this excerpt from *Phoebe's Shakespeare Arranged for Children* would have it, "Portia was so generous and kind that she didn't care how much money it cost to get Antonio out of trouble, and make her dear Bassanio happy" (Gordon 90).

Undoubtedly, the most commonly expressed anxiety about Portia concerned her role as a lawyer, usually taking the form of dismissive references to the character's participation in Antonio's trial. Anna Jameson, in *Characteristics of Women*, claimed that Portia "would rather owe the safety of Antonio to anything rather than the legal quibble with which her cousin Bellario has armed her, and which she reserves as a last resource" (13). While T. Duff Barnett argued that Portia "breaks through the law by a quibble, which strikes us as being rather clever, coming from one we know to be a woman" (9).

The prevalence of this attitude is, to some measure, suggested by a parodic extract from the trial scene, which appeared in *Punch* magazine in May 1900. Here Shylock and the presiding Magistrate improvise a masculine conspiracy to frustrate Portia out of the courtroom by the constant interruption of her case on the basis of legal technicalities. When Portia begins her address with the words "Jew, though justice be thy plea, consider this—," Shylock objects to being "addressed as Jew." When the court upholds the objection, Portia is forced to apologize and start again. When she begins her appeal a second time, the magistrate objects to her alluding to the limitations of justice, and Portia is once again forced to abandon her line of argument. When she begins a third time, the magistrate breaks in to say that he is having trouble following her argument, and, when Portia replies that she cannot conduct her case in the face of constant interruptions, he reprimands her for impropriety in addressing the bench. In the end Portia is forced to retire "in the interests of her client" and "sits down in a huff" as the curtain falls (*Punch* 2/5/1900, 320).

As the possibility of "lady lawyers" may have begun to seem less comical and less remote, the issue was debated with increasing hostility. Marcus Reed, in an essay entitled "Is Portia Possible?" saw the prospect of female advocates as an unambiguous threat to the social order. Although he tried to dismiss the force that Portia, as a symbol, could conceivably mobilize—"one woman-at-arms does not constitute a battalion"—he nevertheless believed that "as a portent and a warning we of the twentieth century have to reckon with her" (375). Like earlier commentators, Reed was eager to dispel any sense of Portia's having secured Antonio's safety by means of legitimate ingenuity. He argued that Portia's was a case of beginner's luck, that she merely "hit upon a flaw, as a junior sometimes does when discovering that a troublesome document is not stamped" (377), and, further, that "not even before Mr. Justice Shallow can Shakespeare have experienced such shocking irregularities" (378). But beyond these familiar gestures of dismissal, for Reed, Portia's attractiveness and moral authority embodied a serious threat to the public/private divide. As he himself put it: "Cross-examination is an ordeal from which every man recoils with horror; who could contemplate with equanimity the possibility of introducing it into the home circle?" (381).

An even more extreme example of this sort of argument is provided by G. K. Chesterton in an essay entitled "Shakespeare and the Legal Lady." Here the threat represented by Portia is thoroughly exposed and the hostility with which she is greeted in her role as lawyer at its most extreme:

> Portia is no more a barrister than Rosalind is a boy . . . The whole point of her position is that she is a heroic and magnanimous fraud. She has not taken up the legal profession, or any profession; she has not sought that public duty, or any public duty. Her action, from first to last, is wholly and entirely private. Her motives are not professional but private. Her ideal is not public but private. She acts as much on personal grounds in the Trial Scene as she does in the Casket Scene. She acts in order to save a friend, and especially a friend of the husband whom she loves . . . This is not what is now called the attitude of a public woman; it is certainly not the attitude of a lady lawyer . . . it is emphatically the attitude of a private woman; that much more ancient and powerful thing. (48–49)

The significance of the disruption or crisis of authority being enacted here may, to some extent, be judged by the hectoring tone of Chesterton's response to Portia but especially by the extraordinary gaffe in his opening pronouncement. For, as any Victorian schoolchild would have been quick to point out, in Shakespeare's day Rosalind would indeed have been a boy. But, beyond the treacherous instability of types which this unintended slip beautifully illustrates, what is crucial here is that even in the face of such immense hostility the need to believe in typological femininity persisted. For, despite her unconscionable masquerading, it is, nevertheless, the ideal represented by Portia, the Shakespeare woman, which Chesterton desired after all. While, he wrote, "we do not want the woman who will enter the law court with the solemn sense of a lasting vocation," we still "want a Portia; a woman who will enter it as lightly, and leave it as gladly as she did" (53).

I V

We can see, then, that the imposition of a prescriptive framework for female experience based on the authority of Shakespeare as supreme arbiter of the human condition was simply one of many strategies employed to mitigate the influence of women, who were making incursions into the public sphere in increasing numbers. Like the discourse of civic maternalism, typological discourse about the Shakespeare woman served to domesticate parts of the public sphere, thus securing them against radical change.

But, though my point has been to add late-nineteenth- and early-twentieth-century ideas about women and Shakespeare to the wider network of social phenomena that simultaneously generated and limited opportunities for female social mobility, I have not done so merely to suggest that Victorian bourgeois hegemony was even worse than originally suspected. On the contrary, if there is a point to be made here, it is one about the political and ideological limitations of a discursive construction like the "Shakespeare woman." The character of Portia constituted a site of political struggle precisely because she seemed to occupy both sides of the public/private divide and therefore confounded attempts to maintain a stable and authoritative separation between the two. Although both the apotheosis of Shakespeare and the separation of the public and private spheres are positions associated with the hegemonic culture, with regard to Portia, the two positions were thrown into a contradictory rather than a complementary relation. To put it another way, Portia posed an insoluble problem for late-nineteenth- and early-twentieth-century moral authority because that authority had put all its eggs in Shakespeare's basket, and suddenly he was widely perceived to be valorizing an otherwise virtuous woman's incursion into the public sphere. While Portia was too good not to be appropriated for her exemplary femininity, increasingly, the attitudes and behaviors she displayed were seen, in many respects, to be contesting such an appropriation. You could tell people that Shakespeare's women were exemplary, and you could tell women how and why they ought to read, but you could never anticipate every reading and every counter-appropriation of the cultural icons. And, when nice middle-class girls like Mrs. Knox's Dorothy or the girls from the *Girl's Own Paper* competition learned, too well, to read in the manner of their exemplars and began to exercise their own political investments, we begin to see an authoritative strategy exposing the limits of its own cultural logic.

3   Shylock: The Infamous Secret Jew

I

Despite its deliberate failure to meet the Victorian vogue for spectacular theater,[1] Henry Irving's Lyceum production of *The Merchant of Venice* set "a record without precedent in the annals of the stage" (L. Irving 356). Mounted and rehearsed in the space of three weeks—Irving having opted to avoid "hampering the natural action of the piece with any unnecessary embellishment" (H. Irving, *MV* preface)—the production, which opened on 1 November 1879, ran for seven straight months, or two hundred and fifty consecutive performances. During the course of that season it was estimated that "330,000 people had visited the Lyceum," generating receipts amounting to some fifty-nine thousand pounds (L. Irving 357). Subsequently, Irving revived the production "nearly every season, took it on every tour, played it perhaps a thousand times, and was still playing it the week he died, more than twenty-five years after the first night" (Hughes 227).[2] On 14 February 1880 the fact that *The Merchant* had "for the first time in history [been] played for a hundred nights in succession" (*Theatre* 1/3/80, 188) was celebrated with dinner for three hundred at the Lyceum at a cost of six hundred pounds (L. Irving 357). And nearly ten years after it opened, the production still had enough cachet that Irving was summoned by the Prince of Wales to perform the trial scene from *The Merchant of Venice* along with *The Bells* (also a play about a Jew) on a specially prepared stage at Sandringham. With one minor exception it was the only theatrical entertainment that Queen Victoria had attended in the twenty-eight years since the death of Prince Albert (512).

Undoubtedly, Irving's star status contributed to the success of the production, but there seemed to be more to it than that; the favorable reception of Irving's Shakespearean offerings was by no means assured. He had had only middling results with both *Coriolanus* and *Twelfth Night* (Hughes 226) and was widely considered to have failed outright with *Macbeth* (E. M. Moore 209). Yet, with *The Merchant of Venice,* Irving "made Shakespeare [truly] popular—an achievement of which but few of his predecessors . . . could boast" (*Theatre* 1/12/79, 292). Thus, the phenomenon seems to be one that cannot be accounted for by cult of personality alone. Moreover, the fact that the production "provoked a controversy" over which both Irving's supporters and detractors "took up extreme positions" (Hughes 225) suggests that something else lay at the heart of it all. That something else, without a doubt, was Irving's treatment of the figure of Shylock, for in Henry Irving's Lyceum production of *The Merchant of Venice,* in all but the most literal of senses, Shylock wins the trial.

While aspects of Irving's Shylock were recognizably indebted to theatrical predecessors such as Charles Macklin and Edmund Kean, Irving was considered to have utterly redefined the role. In popular terms he was widely perceived to be "the first star actor to play Shylock for sympathy" (Maude 172). In an earlier age the part of Shylock had been a two-dimensionally villainous one; as a sort of stock evil buffoon, Shylock was traditionally fitted out with a grotesque red wig and made exaggerated gestures meant to convey the immeasurability of his inhumanity and greed. Moreover, in performance a farcical piece entitled *The Jew of Venice* was actually favored over *The Merchant* from the time of the Restoration until 1741, when "Macklin persuaded the management of Drury Lane to restore Shakespeare's text in place of George Granville's adaptation" (J. R. Brown 187). Challenges to this long tradition of farce had been made by sophisticated interpreters who realized that to play the role entirely in this spirit was to diminish its dramatic interest. But Irving had taken this idea further than anyone before him, moving beyond the difference in degree to effect a striking difference in kind. Irving's Shylock

> was venerable, lonely, grieved, austere: he moved with
> pride and grace; his humour was coldly cynical, rather

> than sardonic; his thought was meditative, not sullen,
> and his anger was white and tense; in defeat he called
> forth pity and awe. (194)

In other words, under Irving's direction *The Merchant of Venice* had ceased to be a comedy and, as one worried critic noted, "foster[ed] the delusion that the play is a tragedy" (*Athenæum* 8/11/79, 605), with Shylock emerging "as something very like a tragic hero" (Hughes 226). To viewers of the Lyceum production, "as in the writing, so in the acting of the play, the first and highest merit . . . [was] the presentation of its tragical element" (E. R. R., "Henry" 16).

It is sometimes suggested that Irving's sympathetic portrayal of the Jew was opportunistic in that he had no choice but to dispense with the traditional histrionic reading of Shylock, since he was not particularly robust and therefore had "not sufficient physical force for such clamorous exhibitions" (Cook 224). An observer at rehearsals for the production once claimed that, although Irving "'shot' for Shakespeare's Shylock," he found that "at least two of the scenes were beyond his powers," forcing him to "develop . . . a 'Shylock' he *could* compass" (Barnes 104). This seems unlikely at best. There were plenty of dramatic moments in Irving's repertoire which required physical force, and discussion of his intentions for the role of Shylock was ongoing for years after the production first opened.[3]

Similarly, claims that Irving's sympathetic Shylock "grew less sympathetic over the years" may be dispatched (J. Gross 141).[4] A review of the 1887 London revival of *The Merchant* confirms that, in the long term, Irving stood his ground. "Mr. Irving's view of the character of Shylock and his subtle appeals for sympathy on the Jew's behalf," the reviewer wrote, "remain of course unchanged. Right or wrong, his is a noble ideal of the part, and he is not likely in any way to lower it" (review [Enthoven]). Indeed, at times Irving's determination to play Shylock as he had developed him at the Lyceum was cause for consternation. On his American tour of 1883 Irving felt that, though the critics consistently applauded his performance, audiences were somewhat taken aback.[5] Joseph Hatton has noted that American spectators expected "in his Shylock a very hard, grim, and cruel Jew":

> Many persons hinted as much to him before they saw his
> impersonation of this much-discussed character . . . Sin-
> gularly sensitive about the feelings of his audiences, and
> accustomed to judge them as keenly as they judge him,
> he fancied . . . [they] were not stirred as they had been
> by his other work in response to his efforts as Shylock.
> (262–63)

Irving himself expressed the fear that the audiences were not with
him:

> I always feel, in regard to this play, that they do not
> quite understand what I am doing. They only responded
> at all . . . where Shylock's rage and mortification get the
> better of his dignity. (Qtd. in ibid. 263)

Hatton sought to reassure Irving by pointing out that audiences
were so strongly accustomed to a histrionic Shylock that they were
"probably a little disappointed" by a "view of the part [which] for-
bids anything like . . . the strident characteristics of most other Shylocks" (263–64). Irving was unwavering in his reply:

> I never saw Kean's Shylock, nor Phelps's, nor, indeed,
> anyone's. But I am sure Shylock was not a low person; a
> miser and usurer, certainly, but a very injured man . . . I
> felt that my audience to-night had quite a different opin-
> ion, and I once wished the house had been composed
> entirely of Jews. I would like to play Shylock to a Jewish
> audience. (264)

Yet, while the production was an unprecedented popular success,
for Irving's antagonists there was still plenty to fault. It was suggested, for example, that the physical mannerisms and affectations of
speech displayed by Shylock were not the product of inspired interpretation but were, in fact, simply Irving's own. Both Irving and
Ellen Terry, one critic observed, "have strange mannerisms; they
never divest themselves of them, and hence . . . are successful where
the parts . . . they play lend themselves to mannerisms . . ." (*Truth*
6/11/79, 568). *Punch*'s theater critic liked the production and so "dis-

miss[ed] Mr. Irving's peculiarities of gait and utterance with . . . [the] remark that they are [at least] less noticeable in *Shylock* than in any part in which I have hitherto seen him" (*Punch* 15/11/79, 225). While George Bernard Shaw, not a fan, summed up the general objection by saying that "the truth is that he [Irving] has never in his life conceived or interpreted the characters of any author except himself" (Shaw, *Dramatic Opinions* 56). The most strenuous objections to Irving's *Merchant of Venice,* however, were reserved for his editorial treatment of the text.

Irving's acting version of the play reduces Shakespeare's text by approximately 25 percent, cutting nearly six hundred lines. Some critics have argued that this was a conventional and logistically motivated editorial intervention, that Irving's text was simply based on Charles Kean's published version of 1858, and that all Irving did was reduce the number of scene changes and eliminate material that failed to advance the plot significantly (Hughes 227). Some of Irving's detractors, however, have argued to the contrary that the cuts he made to the text of *The Merchant of Venice* were anything but superficial. Irving "does not merely cut plays," it was said, "he disembowels them" (Shaw, *Dramatic Opinions* 55). And in this case what Irving's antagonists claimed he did was excise "passages [and]—indeed, whole scenes—which tended to discredit Shylock" (E. M. Moore 203). While these objections to Irving's textual alterations are often questionable insofar as they take the form of ad hominem attacks on a man arrogant enough to have tampered with Shakespeare's text, they do nevertheless raise an interesting question.[6] In isolation, eliminating gratuitous remarks about Shylock's evil nature or reducing the amount of raving about the loss of his ducats would not be gestures drastic enough to alter the play radically. But, in combination with a staging strategy that made Shylock the center of attention and a use of stage business which mitigated the conventional crudity of many of his remaining lines, these cuts *can* be seen as part of a systematic transformation of the text. Whether one approves or disapproves of Irving's editorial conduct, its overall effect was, clearly, to tender an account of Shylock which valorized the character's sufferings rather than confirmed his status as an object of scorn.

The two most obvious alterations Irving made to his acting version of *The Merchant of Venice* were that, first, he consolidated the scenes involving Portia's suitors, pretty clearly in order to reduce the number of scene changes; and, second, predictably, he edited out virtually all references to sex. The first group of changes has no obvious effect on Shylock's part unless one considers that cutting back on Portia's speeches increases proportionally the amount of time given over to Shylock, while the second eliminates only the small handful of insults against the Jew which are bawdy in addition to being racial. But several outstanding alterations fall into neither of these categories and, for a number of reasons, suggest that something more than directorial pragmatism or prevailing standards of good taste may well have been at stake. For, although they are extremely limited in terms of the number of lines they constitute and could hardly be described as essential to the narrative, these passages, as I shall argue, could have attacked the very foundations of Irving's monumental success. All three of these passages concern Shylock's relationship to his daughter, Jessica.

In order of their appearance the relevant omissions consist of all of act 2, scene 3, which is only twenty-one lines long and includes a brief exchange between Jessica and the clown Launcelot Gobbo; act 2, scene 8, lines 12–24, which is a conversation between two minor characters; and act 3, scene 1, lines 22–37, which is a continuation of this same conversation, which by this time includes Shylock. The impact of the absence of these lines, however, is best appreciated if the passages are considered in terms of their content rather than their chronology, so I will begin by considering the latter two passages first.

The first part of the conversation between Salerio and Solanio (friends of Antonio) recounts Shylock's discovery that he has been robbed and abandoned by his daughter:

> *Solanio:*
> I never heard a passion so confused,
> So strange, outrageous, and so variable
> As the dog Jew did utter in the streets:
> "My daughter! O my ducats! O my daughter!

> Fled with a Christian! O my Christian ducats!
> Justice! The law! My ducats and my daughter!
> A sealèd bag, two sealèd bags of ducats,
> Of double ducats, stol'n from me by my daughter!
> And jewels, two stones, two rich and precious stones,
> Stol'n by my daughter! Justice! Find the girl!
> She hath the stones upon her and the ducats!"
>
> *Salerio:*
> Why, all the boys in Venice follow him,
> Crying his stones, his daughter, and his ducats.

Of this exchange Irving retains only the first six lines, therefore editing out both the belabored farce of Shylock's apparent inability to distinguish between his ducats and his daughter and Salerio's description of the spectacle of the anguished Shylock taunted and pursued by "all the boys in Venice." The effect of this is, arguably, considerable, since, by ending the exchange as he does, Irving effectively replaces a raving burlesque with the cynical reporting of what now appears to be a comparatively sympathetic, rational, and not unwarranted call by Shylock for "Justice! The Law! My ducats and my daughter!"

The second passage follows from the previous exchange but now includes the presence of Shylock, who confronts the two men about their having known of his daughter's intended flight:

> *Shylock:*
> You knew, none so well, none so well as you, of my
>   daughter's flight.
> *Salerio:*
> That's certain. I for my part knew the tailor that made
>   the wings she flew withal.
> *Solanio:*
> And Shylock for his own part knew the bird was
>   fledged, and then it is the complexion of them all to
>   leave the dam.
> *Shylock:*
>   She is damned for it.

Salerio:
That's certain, if the devil may be her judge.
Shylock:
My own flesh and blood to rebel!
Solanio:
Out upon it, old carrion! Rebels it at these years?
Shylock:
I say my daughter is my flesh and blood.
Salerio:
There is more difference between thy flesh and hers
than between jet and ivory, more between your
bloods than there is between red wine and Rhenish

. . .

In this instance Irving cuts everything after Shylock's exclamation "My own flesh and blood to rebel!" and moves directly to the discussion of Antonio's losses at sea which follows. While the excised material might seem merely to prolong the already well-established exchange of hostilities between the Venetians and the Jew, it becomes apparent under scrutiny that the omission of the half-dozen lines significantly alters the exchange. For to end on Shylock's lament for his faithless daughter is to construct the issue as one of female disobedience, as a crisis of gender, while to end on Salerio's denial of the legitimacy of Shylock's paternal claim—"There is more difference between thy flesh and hers than between jet and ivory, more between your bloods than there is between red wine and Rhenish"—is to introduce the question of race.

If we look to the final omission from the text, the matter becomes even more explicit, as Jessica considers the twin evils of female disobedience and racial disavowal and in so doing raises the prospect of something more harrowing than either, namely, miscegenation:

Alack, what heinous sin is it in me
To be ashamed to be my father's child.
But though I am a daughter to his blood,
I am not to his manners, O Lorenzo,
If thou keep promise, I shall end this strife,
Become a Christian and thy loving wife.

Whatever the personal intentions of a theatergoer at the time, the experience of watching Irving's *Merchant of Venice* could hardly do less than bring to mind two of the most prominent social crises of the day. The first, as we saw in the previous chapter, is embodied in the figure of Portia and concerns the increasing claims of women over their futures and their social mobility. The second, embodied in the figure of Shylock, evokes the specter of race—the stranger in our midst. The importance of Jessica, as these omissions from the text show, is that she is the figure in which these crises of race and gender are most provocatively manifest for being most perilously entwined. And yet Jessica is an extremely difficult character to pursue, from a historical perspective, because the evidence of attitudes toward her tends to be circumstantial rather than direct. Nevertheless, I would argue, she is pivotal in many ways, and appreciating her importance means that we need to understand not just what people were saying about her but also why they were saying so little when they were saying anything at all.

One obvious difficulty in approaching the character of Jessica is the extent to which she is overshadowed, legendarily, by her larger-than-life father but even more so by the cult of Portia, a difficulty considerably compounded by the popular association of the two characters with figures as charismatic in their own rights as Henry Irving and Ellen Terry. Indeed, in Irving's production the sidelining of Jessica was clearly reinforced by the casting of the role. For at the Lyceum the part was played by an actress named Alma Murray, who was apparently so young and undistinguished that a reviewer for *Blackwood's Magazine* complained of its having been "regarded of as so little importance as to be intrusted to . . . [a young lady] who would be weak in the smallest of comediettas" (12/79, 651). As we shall see, this marginalization of Jessica served a particular function in relation to Irving's production, but the character's diminished status was by no means limited to that context alone.

In a literary culture so heavily dominated by character criticism, for example, Jessica was seldom the focus of substantial interest in her own right. Partly this was due to the prevailing conventions, which tended to focus on leading roles, and partly to the associated bias in favor of characters who lent themselves to the endorsement of an exemplary nature. Thus, when she is acknowledged, it is often just in passing or in an aside as the lesser party in an unfavorable comparison with Portia. Anna Jameson's reference to Jessica simply as one of "the other female characters of 'The Merchant of Venice'" who deserves our notice, primarily because "something of the intellectual brilliance of Portia is reflected on [her]" is fairly typical (39). It's not that Jessica is seen to be utterly unworthy of attention. Indeed, "in any other play," Jameson consoled her readers, and,

> in any other companionship than that of the matchless Portia, Jessica would make a very beautiful heroine of herself . . . Nothing can be more . . . elegant than the scenes between her and Lorenzo . . . Every sentiment she utters interests us for her . . . And the enthusiastic and generous testimony to the superior graces and accomplishments of Portia comes with a peculiar grace from her lips. (39–40)

The most commonly held perception of Jessica, then, was that, if she were herself short on virtue, at least she could detect it in others. "One of the things we like best in Jessica," one commentator wrote, "is her genuine admiration of Portia . . . It augurs the development of her own character . . . into something ampler and more responsible" (Verity xxxiii). Helena Faucit held a similar view. That Jessica can, "despite her training, appreciate goodness and virtue," she wrote, "may be inferred from what she says of Portia" (Martin 36).

Occasionally, Jessica would be acknowledged for other reasons, but this was usually done with considerable resentment—much as one would acknowledge the winner of a door prize—for being the character who gets to have the beautiful poetry of the last act of *The Merchant of Venice* spoken to her, although she has done nothing special to deserve it. As one particularly peeved reviewer put it, Jessica was someone "to whom one always grudges the loveliest love-lines ever spoken" (qtd. in Hughes 232).

Where we do find evidence of a less backhanded interest in Jessica, suggestively, the emphasis is often placed on the utility of her part rather than on its moral content or iconic significance. In a society intent on emphasizing the structural perfection of Shakespeare's plays, in other words, one way of dealing with Jessica was clearly to relegate her to a role that, if morally treacherous, was at least structurally recuperable for linking the casket and bond stories together or for providing the contrast needed to develop other characters. Thus, the Jessica-Lorenzo plot was seen as "assisting" the main plot by "bridging over the three months' interval between the signing of the bond and its becoming due" or by "occupy[ing] some of the superfluous characters of the Merchant's story" (Barnett 10). Similarly, its relation to the "main drift of the drama" was explained in terms of its furnishing "a contrast to the graver love-story of Bassanio and Portia" or illuminating the character of Shylock, giving greater insight into his "avarice," his "motive in pressing for the execution of the bond," and showing him "in his domestic relations, which we would not otherwise see" (Verity 119).

On all counts, then, it was difficult for Jessica to compete. She could hardly command the interest of a Portia or a Shylock, and, however key she might appear with hindsight, from a late Victorian perspective she was notable mainly for her failings, "properly kept subordinate" (Jameson 39) and recuperable only through her structural utility and awareness of the superiority of those around her. But, this being said, there is evidence that points in another direction and which suggests that there were aspects of the character that could not be so easily dismissed. For, despite her obvious and deliberate marginalization in popular attitudes, in pedagogy and literary scholarship, but especially in Irving's high-profile theatrical production, there is a palpable anxiety about Jessica which far outweighs her ostensible lack of importance.

One place we immediately get a sense of this is in discussions of Jessica which take place in the notes accompanying school editions of *The Merchant of Venice,* possibly because this is a forum in which moral issues would be difficult to ignore. And here we begin to get a sense of the true depth of feeling associated with the character and of the terrible dilemmas her situation must have posed for a late Victorian audience. Specifically, one is struck by the resonant and highly contested way in which the theme of public accountability extended beyond the parameters of Shylock's story to encompass that of his daughter, the notion of judgment figuring centrally throughout.

"Jessica's conduct stands at the bar of judgment," wrote one editor. "Although she describes her home as a hell, and from Shylock's nature that can well be believed, there could not be baser ingratitude in a Jewess than to steal her father's jewels and money, and take flight with a Christian" (Crook lv–lvi). Or, contrastingly, "Jessica is not to be judged by any present-day standard of morality," wrote another:

> The poet himself evidently intended her failings to be regarded with much leniency, and we must endeavour therefore to view her in the light of a . . . lively young girl, driven to rebellion by the oppression of her father and the joylessness of her life at home. Otherwise we shall be unable to justify such glaring transgressions as the appropriation of her father's ducats and her desertion of him in his old age. (Wood, Manuals 16–17)

Clearly, the difficulty with the story of Jessica was that it presented a litany of what to a late Victorian audience would have been highly charged moral concerns in an uncomfortably complicated set of relations to one another—female disobedience, racial and religious disloyalty, the effects of an unsuitable domestic environment, premeditated deception, conversion, and, of course, miscegenation.[7] And, like the question of Portia's feminism or lack of it, it thus occasioned substantial disagreement about Shakespeare's intentions in representing the character and her actions as he did.

Sometimes, Jessica's disregard for family loyalty is seen to be mitigated by her genuine feeling for her lover, so that, while she is censured for not even making the "pretence of being a dutiful daughter to the Jew, whom she deceives with the lightest conscience," she is redeemed for being genuinely in love with Lorenzo" (Wood, Manuals 16–17). But at other times no such allowance is made, and, despite "all her . . . love of Lorenzo," she is declared to be "but a heartless beauty" (Meiklejohn 4). Likewise, while Jessica's Jewishness is in some cases seen to be enacted through her disobedience, at others it is an attribute made tragic by actions declared to be uncharacteristic of this normally loyal race. Thus, we are told in one instance that "there could not be baser ingratitude in a Jewess than to steal her father's jewels and money and take flight with a Christian" (Crook lv–lvi), while in another we are assured that "to rob her father of his ducats and precious stones . . . was a touch of Judaism too much for Christian forgiveness" (Meiklejohn 4). In another still, Jessica's mercurial racial identification itself becomes the key to her redemption, since, it is claimed, "she is not a Jewess in heart and feelings . . . and will readily become a Christian when she marries her lover" (Wood, Manuals 16–17).

It is perhaps not surprising, then, that Henry Irving opted to sever rather than untangle the Gordian knot of racial and domestic affiliations which Jessica brings to the text of *The Merchant of Venice*. For it is harder to imagine anything that would more immediately provoke a late Victorian audience than the suggestion that a faithless daughter could become a faithful wife; that the endowment of manners could be distinguished from the inheritance of blood; that a Jew of discreditable family could become a Christian; and, perhaps most disturbingly, that, in spite of it all, Jessica was a serious marriage prospect by virtue of her dowry, regardless of how it was obtained. What is crucial to recognize here is that in this marginalized and, as we have seen, easily excised character, whose own shortcomings serve primarily to endorse our adoration of the heroine, is constituted a site of significant struggle. And what I am arguing about Henry Irving's *Merchant of Venice* is that its fantastic attractions must be understood in terms of the conflicts and social anxieties it strategically excised when it selectively redefined the representation of Shylock's relationship to his daughter.

Irving's phenomenally successful bid for Shylock as tragic hero is substantially underwritten by his portrayal of the character as a benevolent patriarch betrayed by his thankless child. Audiences saw a Shylock who was "tenderly attached to his daughter" (Hawkins 194), a father who loved Jessica "with no ignoble love" and "feels bitterly her desertion of him and her renunciation of the old faith" (F. Marshall, "Introduction" 251). In order to gain this effect Irving had to play quite deliberately against the text, even after having excised so many lines. And he apparently did so without reserve:

> after Shylock's outburst in III, i, "I would my daughter
> were dead at my foot," etc. (lines 88 ff.), Irving paused,

> hid his face in his hands, and murmured an anguished
> "No, no, no, no!" . . . in the subsequent self-pitying lines
> on his losses, he opened his robe and smote himself con-
> tinually, slowly, and heavily on his bare breast . . . after
> Jessica's elopement . . . the curtain . . . rose on Shylock
> silently walking in the moonlight across the bridge and
> deserted streets to his home. Originally, the curtain fell
> as he reached his door, later only after he had knocked
> several times. (E. M. Moore 201–2)[8]

While the gender politic is thus exploited in order to gain sympathy
for Shylock, the racial element is, for the same reason, deliberately
downplayed. Irving all but eradicated any suggestion of the Jew's
conventionally anticipated obsession with money. Indeed, "to one
alert listener at an early performance . . . [Shylock] spoke 'with the
reflective air of a man to whom money means very little.'" This was
apparently more than Irving had intended, and he was compelled to
amend his reading of the character in order to convey at least the fact
that money was indeed important to Shylock "as a shield against persecution" (Hughes 230). This greatly modified relation of the character to money was something that many viewers were moved to comment upon. Rather than endorse the customary view that Shylock's
greed was an inevitable manifestation of his racial identity and a quid
pro quo for the play, commentators sought, instead, the mitigating
circumstances that had led Shylock to be so. "His avarice," it was
argued, was "a vice forced upon him by circumstances" (Hawkins,
"Shylock" 194). And, they said, "that it was not personal avarice is . . .
proved when Shylock scorns thrice his principal proffered to cancel
his bond" (Conway 836). Moreover, the sort of reading which sought
and found in the character an impressive display of family feeling further identified Shylock as the jealously maligned self-made man. According to some, Shylock cared about money

> not for the pleasures it can purchase for him, nor with
> that narrow-minded vanity in the sense of possession
> which the mere miser feels; but rather because it is the
> evidence of his own thrift and industry, the . . . witness,

in one respect at least, to his superiority over the Christians who despise and persecute him. (Marshall, "Introduction" 251)

We can see, then, the extent to which Irving's sympathetic portrayal of Shylock depends on a disavowal of race mobilized by the vilification of Jessica. To have allowed the racial question to stand would have been to engage the single element most liable to undermine Irving's carefully wrought appeal. The stage having thus been set, the tragic hero was now free to play out his final moments of glory in the trial scene. For the Jew, safely divested of all but the most sentimental attributes of race, was now eligible to occupy high moral ground.

Drawing on Charles Kean's conception of a diagonal staging, "the design for the trial scene fulfilled the major function of centring the action on Shylock" (Foulkes, "Staging" 317). It was here that Irving was most liberal with his use of innovative stage business, introducing "a crowd of Jews . . . to emphasize the . . . persecution theme" (E. M. Moore 202), and that the originality of his performance was at its most striking. "Unlike other Shylocks, Irving made his strongest effects in the Trial Scene. Here his dignity had its full scope" (J. R. Brown 194):

> At the end of Portia's verdict he dropped the scales and stood as though mesmerized . . . his lips murmured incoherent words as his whole body resumed a dreamy, motionless attitude. When Shylock grasped the severity of his sentence, his eyelids became heavy as though he was hardly able to lift them and his eyes became listless and vacant. The words "I am not well . . . " were the plea of a doomed man to be allowed to leave the court and to die in utter loneliness. But Gratiano's ill-timed jibe governed Shylock's exit. He turned. Slowly and steadily the Jew scanned his tormentor from head to foot, his eyes resting on the Italian's face with concentrated scorn. The proud rejection of insult and injustice lit up his face for a moment, enough for the audience to

> feel a strange relief in knowing that, in that glance, Shy-
> lock had triumphed. (L. Irving, qtd in. E. M. Moore
> 202–3)

The strength of Irving's performance in the trial scene was so overwhelming that it generated difficulties for the other actors and, in particular, for his co-star, Ellen Terry. Terry's own popularity had been greatly enhanced by her debut performance of Portia in the Bancroft's production of *The Merchant of Venice* four years earlier. Visually stunning but otherwise undistinguished, the production had been praised mainly for Terry's performance, and, undoubtedly, this was something audiences had in mind when they purchased their tickets for the Lyceum *Merchant of Venice*. But Irving's Shylock was heroic to the extent that it necessitated a radical revision of Ellen Terry's carefully thought out and established interpretation of her role. In effect, Irving's Shylock made Ellen Terry's Portia impossible. "I am," she wrote, "of the mind that Portia in the trial scene ought to be very quiet . . . But as Henry's Shylock was quiet, I had to give it up. His heroic saint was splendid, but it wasn't good for Portia" (qtd. in Taylor 191).

Another objection arising out of Irving's portrayal of Shylock in the trial scene was that the representation of the Jew so altered people's expectations of the play that it became virtually unrecognizable. Although his Shylock was "undoubtedly a great piece of acting," it was seen to be "un-Shakespearian if not anti-Shakespearian" (Jones, qtd. in Sprague, "Irving" 111). "There was no question . . . of a bad Shylock or a good Shylock . . . when . . . [Irving's] own creation came into conflict with Shakespeare's he simply played in flat contradiction to the lines and acted Shakespeare off the stage" (Shaw, *Dramatic Opinions* 56). As one anonymous reviewer put it, "Before a persecuted Hebrew prophet for hero, a dull ill-mannered Christian for villain, and an incomparable Portia flinging in her lot with the might-is-right party, Shakespeare retired discomfited" (qtd. in Taylor 191). These sorts of opinions were far from quibbling. Where you stood in relation to Irving's Shylock was a matter upon which people staked their personal reputations. And on at least two notable occasions prominent members of the audience went to extreme lengths to dissociate themselves from Irving's reading of the play.

The first such incident actually took place at the dinner celebrating Irving's one hundredth performance of *The Merchant*. Lord Houghton, known as an after-dinner speaker and seated to Irving's right, had been asked, according to custom, to propose a toast. Rather than inviting the assembled guests to join him in celebrating the achievements of Irving and his company, however, Lord Houghton reprimanded Irving "for following the example of some contemporary historians in white-washing and rehabilitating the established villains of the drama." "He for one could not accept Shylock as 'a gentleman of the Hebrew race with the manners of a Rothschild'" (qtd. in L. Irving 354–55).

Even more striking, perhaps, was a comparable incident involving John Ruskin. After attending a performance of *The Merchant*, Ruskin had been invited to meet Irving backstage. At that meeting Ruskin praised Irving's performance, describing it as "noble, tender, and true." The compliment was somehow relayed to Clement Scott, editor of *Theatre* magazine, and found its way into the pages of that publication a short time later. By the next day, however, Ruskin had decided that he had only praised Irving out of politeness and thus wrote to the actor in order to express his views "with more accuracy and frankness." What those views consisted of, primarily, was the belief that Irving's Shylock was, precisely, un-Shakespearean, or, as Ruskin put it, "not . . . in harmony with his [Shakespeare's] design" (L. Irving 346). But this retraction was conveyed too late to stop the compliment he had paid Irving from appearing in the pages of *Theatre,* and Ruskin was so vexed by this that he once again felt compelled to reply. Here the story becomes truly baroque, for, while Ruskin was clearly incensed about being represented as approving of Irving's *Merchant of Venice* and was accordingly anxious to retrieve his reputation, he suddenly declared himself to be in poor health, too ill to carry on the debate, and so engaged a Mr. Laister to continue the correspondence with Irving on his behalf. In the event Laister wrote to Irving, communicating Ruskin's views, and it is worth noting here the more specific meanings that the phrase "not in harmony with Shakespeare's design" began to reveal once Ruskin had handed over the disagreeable task of being specific on the subject of Shylock to someone else. "You are probably aware," Laister wrote,

> that the Play in question, as revived, has given rise to a vast deal of public teaching, the moral of which Mr. Ruskin and others greatly deplore; and he naturally desires to correct any wrong impression which the unqualified publication of the paragraph in *The Theatre* might create. (Qtd. in L. Irving 348)

Ruskin had told Laister about the original letter he had sent to Irving and directed him to request that "*the whole* of that letter" be published in the *Theatre* as a retraction. Irving's response, not surprisingly, was to "decline to enter into correspondence with a stranger" and to inquire why "Mr. Ruskin . . . does not write to me in person . . . if he has any communication to make to me" (349). Despite these considerable difficulties, a version of Ruskin's letter finally did appear in *Theatre,* allowing him to have his say. And what he actually did say at that point was: "I entirely dissent (and indignantly as well as entirely) from his [Irving's] general reading and treatment of the play." Furthermore, Ruskin went on to suggest that anyone interested in a fuller rendering of his views on Shakespeare's meaning in *The Merchant of Venice* should consult his essay "Munera Pulveris," in which he argued that "[the inhumanity of mercenary commerce] is the ultimate lesson which the leader of English intellect meant for us" (*Theatre* 1/3/80 169).

Such incidents are telling, particularly in light of the fact that, for most of the hundreds of thousands of spectators attending the Lyceum production, Irving's *Merchant of Venice* was a triumph and Shylock's exit from the trial scene "the crowning glory" of the play; for most it was the ultimate tragic exit, "and many of the audience actually wept" (Hughes 238). At one point during the opening run Irving cut the entire fifth act, thus ending the play with Shylock's exit from the trial. While the piece was only acted in this form for two months, in order to allow Ellen Terry to star in a one-act version of *Iolanthe* appearing on the same bill, the gesture gave rise to an apocryphal legend. Whenever Henry Irving played *The Merchant of Venice,* people liked to believe, he played it that way.

But even more powerful than the objection that Irving's Shylock was un-Shakespearean was the fear that it was not. For, if Irving were right, then the bard of Avon might indeed have written the play as a plea for toleration toward the Jews.[9] Moreover, once the conventions governing dominant representations of Jews had been exposed and the possibility raised that Shylock was neither grotesque nor merely a clown, the attention of the Victorian public was forced away from the artificiality of the theater to the world outside its doors. The problem with Irving's sympathetic Shylock was that it tended to dispel Victorian nostalgia for the Elizabethan age, leaving nothing in its wake but the threat of internationalism and the increasing pressures of modernity. It admitted the presence of Jews in modern English society and asked, in a way that could not be ignored: If Shylock were not the loathsome and primitive buffoon he had long been held to be, then who was he? How did he get here? And where did he come from?

The simplest and perhaps, for that reason, one of the most popular answers to these questions was that Shylock had come from "somewhere else." The character was declared to be manifestly un-English, the invention of foreigners, undoubtedly having gained entry into England by unconventional means like a dangerous foundling taken in by an unsuspecting English couple. "The Germans have started a theory," one critic wrote,

> that in Shylock Shakespeare wished to portray a sort of noble and dignified martyr to popular prejudice, and this nonsense has been still further elaborated by some of our own critics, who ask us to believe that the Jew of Venice is the embodiment of the spirit of toleration. (*Truth* 6/11/79, 569)

Another line of argument contested the sympathetic Shylock by construing him as a logical impossibility, in effect, as an anachronism whose admission to the realm of possibility invidiously altered the terms of the debate. "To say that . . . [Irving's] was the Jew that Shakespeare drew," wrote one commentator, "would be to quote

Pope's doggerel inopportunely." Rather, he argued, "it was the Jew idealized in the light of the modern Occidental reaction against the *Judenhetze,* a Jew already conscious of the Spinozas, the Sidonias, the Disraelis, who were to issue from his loins" (Walkley 136). The un-Shakespearean Shylock altered the balance of power in ways that, up to this point, had been inconceivable, and he rudely exposed the extent to which the inner sanctums of politics and finance had been penetrated by Jews. In the words of one of Irving's first reviewers:

> Irving has . . . impart[ed] to his impersonation . . . the ruling feelings of a Jew such as Shakespeare has drawn . . . [and] these . . . reveal a lofty consciousness such as once manifested to an English constituency by a candidate "descended from a line of Jewish merchants who had . . . told the electors that his ancestors had been princes and statesmen when theirs were staining their bodies with woad." (E. R. R., "Henry" 16)

Yet another response to the question "Who is Shylock, and where did he come from?" was generated in literary-historical circles in which the matter was taken up as a question of genealogy seeking out the origins of Shylock. But, while, in one sense, this was simply the predictable academic response to Henry Irving's "admirable impersonation" of Shylock and the interest it rekindled in a subject that "had long been a bone of contention among critics" (Lee, "Original" 185), in other ways it was more than just another round of debate about literary representations of Jews. As we shall see, the ostensibly editorial task of locating the "original of Shylock" became a search for origins in a number of far-reaching and unforeseen ways, suggesting—at least to a contemporary cultural historian—that the critical exigency here lies not with discovering the historical origins of Shylock but, rather, with examining the motivations of late-nineteenth-century Shakespeareans.

I I

> A Jew, in the dictionary, is one who is descended from the ancient tribes of Judea, or one who is regarded as

descended from that tribe. That's what it says in the dictionary; but you and I know what a Jew is—*One Who Killed Our Lord* . . . All right. I'll clear the air once and for all, and confess. Yes, we did it. I did it, my family. I found a note in my basement. It said: "We killed him. signed, Morty." And a lot of people say to me, "Why did you kill Christ?" . . . We killed him because he didn't want to become a doctor, that's why we killed him.

(Bruce 40–41)

Ruy Lopez, a Jewish Portuguese doctor and personal physician to Elizabeth I, was accused of conspiring to poison the monarch, found guilty, and publicly hanged in June 1594. The affair was widely considered to have inspired both the figures of Shylock and of Marlowe's Barrabas, since it was believed to be roughly contemporaneous with the first productions of both *The Merchant of Venice* and *The Jew of Malta*. While it now seems possible that Lopez was indeed involved in espionage and had, in fact, intended an attempt on the queen's life,[10] what is at issue here is not Lopez's demonstrable innocence or guilt but, rather, the manner in which his story, as it was understood at the time, seized the attention of a number of critics and historians in the latter decades of the nineteenth century. I shall return to those accounts of the Lopez affair later on. For the moment, however, it will be helpful to define the story's parameters and to provide a basis for understanding why it was that people, three hundred years later, wished to find in Lopez a prototype of the figure of Shylock.

Lopez is believed to have settled in England in 1559. He "rapidly reached the highest places in the medical profession in London [and] was the first to hold the office of house physician at St. Bartholomews' Hospital." By 1575 he was listed as one of "the chief London doctors" and shortly afterward served as physician to the household of the Earl of Leicester. In 1586 he was appointed personal physician to Queen Elizabeth, who, in addition to bestowing the honor of his appointment, granted Lopez "a monopoly for the importation of aniseed and sumach into England" (Lee, *Lopez* 132–33). Lopez's success excited a considerable degree of envy, a fact witnessed by the derisory accounts of his rise to public prominence set out in the pamphlets of the day. Gabriel Harvey described him as a man who "by a kind of Jewish practis hath growen to much wealth and sum reputation as well with ye queen herself as with sum of ye greatest Lordes and Ladyes" (qtd. in Lee, *Lopez* 133). One of these lords was the Earl of Essex, whose increasing animosity toward Lopez seems to have been central in contributing to his demise.

Essex attempted to engage Lopez in gathering political intelligence about Spain. Lopez declined, however, and compounded Essex's irritation by disclosing details of his activities to the queen. The intrigue that ensued is unimaginably complicated and cannot be entered into here, but, in briefest outline, a plot was hatched in which Spanish spies in London were alleged to be conspiring to poison both Queen Elizabeth and Don Antonio of Spain. As alleged conspirators were arrested and made statements under torture or threat of torture, Lopez was brought under suspicion. Essex "insisted on his guilt," and Lopez was imprisoned and tried. "The prosecution was conducted by Sir Edward Coke . . . who described the prisoner as 'a perjured and murdering villain and Jewish doctor, worse than Judas himself.'" After Lopez's conviction the queen "delayed signing the death-warrant for three months" but was ultimately unable to prevent his execution. Even in death, however, to those at court Lopez appeared to maintain his privileged vicinity to the center of power; "the queen is said to have worn at her girdle until death . . . [a] jewel given to Lopez by Philip of Spain" (Lee, *Lopez* 134).

There are two powerful metaphors at work in the story of Dr. Lopez which merit particular attention. One is the metaphor of Marranism, or the secret profession of Judaism, to which I will return. The other is the metaphor of the Jewish doctor in an otherwise Jewless state.

At the time that Lopez was appointed personal physician to Queen Elizabeth, England had been, technically speaking, Jewless since the year 1290, when the Jews were expelled by King Edward I. In fact, Jews had been secretly settling in England at least since their expulsion from Spain in 1492. More to the point, however, as Gil Harris has noted, in acquiring a Jewish doctor for the monarch, England was participating in a long-standing if "seemingly inexplicable tradition" of popes and Christian rulers "receiving care from Jewish physicians" (8). This custom posed more than just the obvious paradox of entrusting the well-being of the head of state or the head of the church to an individual whose entire race had been banished for political and spiritual undesirability. For, renowned as they were for their skills in curative medicine, Jews were also commonly believed to be experts in the art of poisoning; and Jewish physicians, it was assumed, participated in a secret but nonetheless somehow universally acknowledged program of "diabolical revenge against Christianity."[11] "The Vienna Faculty of Medicine believed that a private code adhered to by Jewish physicians obliged them to murder one patient in ten [while,] according to Spanish authorities, the figure was one in five" (7). The very Jewishness of the physician was seen to embody "semi-magical properties" (8) so that, absurdly, the attraction of the Jewish court physician was precisely the danger he or she brought to bear. Harris's analysis of the phenomenon is persuasive. The point in employing a Jewish doctor, he says, was that, "as in a modern-day vaccination," the presence of a Jewish physician at court enacted a regulated exposure of the body politic to a toxic substance (9). If Jews could not be hermetically excluded from the state, then at least their secret and powerful presence within it could be harnessed and controlled. When England purged Dr. Lopez from its body politic, it reasserted the integrity of its political boundaries, expelling what was undesirable while appropriating the doctor's seemingly ominous powers for itself.

The issues surrounding Lopez's Marranism are similarly intriguing. Marranos were enforced Jewish converts to Christianity. Yet, though these people were, strictly speaking, fully Christian, in practice the term was perceived to be "synonymous with the secret profession of Judaism" (Lipman 1), and the case of Dr. Lopez typifies the Marranos' habitual fate. For, while he had "been baptized, and was a professing member and communicant of the Church of England," according to his enemies "he was said to be no Christian at heart" (Dimock 440–41). On the scaffold Lopez protested his innocence, affirming, up until the moment of his death, his loyalty to church and queen. Yet, though

> with his last words he emphatically insisted that he had
> loved his mistress better than Christ Jesus . . . coming
> from one believed to be in secret a Jew by religion as he
> was by race, this did but excite the derisive laughter of
> the multitude. (469)

Of all the ways in which Lopez's story prefigures the institutional
anti-Semitism of late-nineteenth- and early-twentieth-century commentators on Shakespeare, it is the issue of his Marranism, I would
argue, that comes closest to providing a root metaphor for it all. It is
a metaphor that I would now like to explore.

   In Spain during the Middle Ages Christians, Muslims, and Jews
coexisted successfully, if at times uneasily, for centuries. With the
Catholic reconquest of Spain, however, the social position of the
Jews became increasingly difficult to resolve. For, while Jewish participation in the consolidation of the Catholic state was, on the one
hand, considered to be crucial, on the other, it was an enduring
point of convergence for popular resentment. On the most basic
level the allegiance of the Jews had to be secured in order to ensure
that they did not side with the Muslims, but their position was considerably more complex than that. Barred from certain trades and
professions, Jews had tended, historically, to earn their living by the
provision of services and, as a result, possessed administrative and
diplomatic skills that the state was anxious to deploy on its own
behalf. Moreover, as occupants of the cultural space between Muslims and Christians, Jews were particularly well placed to serve as
"intermediaries" in the adaptation of Muslim institutions to Catholic forms of administration (Poliakov 110). But this Jewish participation in the unification of the Catholic state, effective as it was,
gave rise to a dilemma. For, the more successful the mediation and
thus the stronger and more unified the state, the more conspicuous
became the position of Jews as infidels outside the Catholic Church.
And, the more pronounced the infidelity of the Jews seemed, the
more it appeared that there was something nefarious about their
influential position within Spanish society. Over time perceptions of
the social position of Spanish Jews deteriorated into the classic anti-
Semitic trope that conveyed the belief that Jews constituted a privi-

leged urban economic caste who exercised a disproportionate influence within the nation, "earning their living without much labour while sitting on their bottoms" (Bernáldez, qtd. in Kamen, *Spanish* 10). And, not surprisingly, the long-standing oscillation between tolerance toward the Jews and discrimination against them eventually degenerated into one of the most protracted catastrophes in Jewish history, culminating in the Inquisition and the expulsion from Spain.

The mounting hostility toward the Jews in Spain expressed itself in conventional ways. Jews were prohibited from participating in trade and commerce, their social mobility and literal freedom of movement were severely restricted, and they were subject to massacres and innumerable smaller-scale physical attacks. Some official efforts were made to ensure the safety of the Jews, but these were effective only in limited ways and in the short term. Significant numbers of Jews converted to Christianity over the years in order to escape persecution, but, as they tended to maintain their associations with unconverted Jews, it was felt that the menace to the Catholic state endured. Many of the converts "lived close to the Jewish quarter to which they still felt a cultural affinity; they retained traditional characteristics in dress and food . . . [and] some returned actively to the practice of Judaism" (Kamen, *Spanish* 27). In 1492 the situation was declared to be intolerable, and it was decreed that the presence of Jews in Spain would no longer be allowed. In July of that year an ultimatum was issued: submit to conversion or be expelled. Hundreds of thousands of Jews fled, initially mainly to Portugal, where they enjoyed a brief period of security. Unfortunately, this only lasted for five years as one of the conditions of a marriage, negotiated between King Manoel of Portugal and Isabel, daughter of Ferdinand and Isabella of Spain, was that the Jews of Portugal convert to Christianity or face expulsion. The Marranos were those who, rather than suffer the terms of exile, chose to convert to Catholicism and stay in Spain.

Once a Jew had become a convert and was no longer subject to political and religious disabilities, there was nothing to impede his or her progress in Spanish society. Understandably enough then, given that they were now free of long-standing restrictions, converts rapidly made their way into the professions, especially law and medicine, the political and financial administration, the municipal councils, the legislature, the army, the universities, and even the church (Roth 21). Moreover, "commercial agility and a . . . disposition to mutual help . . . put them in the vanguard of the new urban bourgeoisie and, in the next century, of the protocapitalist and entrepreneurial class that was then budding in Spain and Portugal" (Yovel 16–17). But, while this successful absorption of the Marranos into every aspect of life should, at least in theory, have satisfied the terms of the act of homogenization which the Spanish state had so forcefully sought, in fact, it merely recast ancient hostilities. For, where once the objection to their presence lay in the question of religion, it now came to be expressed in terms of blood. The Marranos, it was said, were tainted, inferior, impure.[12] And, like the unconverted Jews before the expulsion, they were considered to be exercising an undue influence over Spanish affairs.

By the mid sixteenth century, for example, "it was reputed that most of the Spanish clergy resident in Rome in search of preferment were of Jewish origin" (Kamen, *Spanish* 22) and that a considerable number of Spanish bishops were, in reality, converted Jews. Wealthy Marranos "intermarried with the highest nobility of the land . . . [so that] within a couple of generations, there was barely a single aristocratic family in Aragon, from the royal house downwards, which was free from the 'taint' of Jewish blood" (Roth 21). The Marranos, or New Christians as they were sometimes called, appeared to have finessed their way "into the heart of Christian society, into the ranks of the aristocracy and the Church" (Kamen, *Spanish* 22). And, willfully blind to the role that the enforced conversions had played in creating this situation, popular prejudice held that an alien infestation was hollowing the nation out from the inside.

What the Marranos found themselves confronting was the paradox of assimilation in its most overt form. For, in choosing to submit to conversion in order to avoid expulsion or death, the Marranos had responded to the tacit assurance conveyed by the state's ultimatum: "Become like us—abandon your difference—and you may be one with us." But assimilation is, precisely, a paradox, and the offer of undifferentiated acceptance is thus, by definition, always falsely tendered. "The more you are like me," says the dominant culture, "the more I know the true value of my power, which you wish to share, and the more I am aware that you are but a shoddy counterfeit, an outsider" (Gilman, *Jewish* 2).

While the church could not officially sanction the shunning of Marranos, since the mass conversions had been undertaken at its behest, and to deny their legitimacy would be to deny its own jurisdiction, in practice there was little if any distinction maintained between Marranos and unconverted Jews. The Franciscan Alfonso de Espina gave voice to a widespread belief when he declared that "there were two types of Jews, public Jews and hidden Jews, and that both had the same nature" (Poliakov 181). Unconverted Jews suddenly seemed preferable, since there was at least little doubt about their identity. The problem with the Marranos was that they claimed to be Christians, which, of course, they were—except that everyone knew that they weren't. Jews outside the church were infidels, but they had been dealt with, expeditiously, by the general expulsion. False Christians, which is to say secret Jews inside the church, however, were heretics, and this was by far the greater menace. It was a situation that only the Inquisition could resolve.

The methods of the Inquisition are well documented, and there would be no point here in reiterating the fate of the Marranos at its hands. What is germane to this discussion, however, is the question of how the Inquisition identified its subjects, for deciphering the secrecy of the Jews and learning to deal with their "inherent duplicity" was, as we shall see, a preoccupation that the Inquisition shared with a great many cultures, late Victorian literary society among them.

Historiographically speaking, the secret life of the Marranos is a subject of considerable debate, but, for the time being, the traditional account of their existence is the one that matters here and runs as follows. Publicly, the Marranos lived as Christians, and while there were some "who had not been over-sincere in their attachment to Judaism, and did not find much difficulty in accommodating themselves . . . to their new religion . . . the vast majority," it was believed, "had accepted Christianity only to escape death, and remained at heart as completely Jewish as they had ever been" (Roth 19):

Outwardly they lived as Christians. They took their children to church to be baptized, though they hastened to
wash off the traces of the ceremony as soon as they
returned home. They would go to the priest to be married, though they were not content with the ceremony
and, in the privacy of their houses, performed another to
implement it . . . Their disbelief in the dogmas of the
Church was notorious, and . . . not always concealed.
They kept all the traditional [Jewish] ceremonies, in
some instances down to the last details. They observed
the Sabbath so far as lay in their power; and it was possible to see, from a height overlooking any city, how many
chimneys were smokeless on that day . . . they married
exclusively amongst themselves . . . In race, in belief, and
. . . in practice, they remained as they had been before
conversion. They were Jews in all but name, and Christians in nothing but form. They were moreover able to
transmit their disbelief to their children, who, though
born in the dominant faith and baptized at birth, were as
little sincere in their attachment to it as their fathers.
(20)

The problem with the Marranos, then, was considered to be twofold,
a fact that is evident in the twin discourses that arose antagonistically
around them and engaged, in tandem, notions of racial predisposition and of the pernicious exploitation of the private sphere. Jews can
never be anything other than Jews, it said. Their race is the most
important thing about them; they cannot form alliances or make
commitments as anything other than Jews.[13] No matter what they
say or do in public, in the privacy of their homes they will revert to
their innate identity. Their participation in public ceremonies and
their declarations of loyalty to persons or institutions outside their
own ranks mean nothing, since at home they will simply wash away
any trace of these commitments and cease to be their public selves.
Jews only marry other Jews. Jews have Jewish children, to whom
they communicate, by both biological and social means, the essence
of deceit.

The reputed cunning and boundlessness of the Marrano conspiracy set the Inquisition a special challenge, for it found the greatest perils in the greatest semblance of order and the truth to be indistinguishable from lies. Thus, the more mundane and normal the behavior of a Marrano, the more likely he or she was to be brought under suspicion. "Edicts of Faith" were issued which "summoned . . . the faithful . . . to denounce to the . . . authorities any person . . . guilty of . . . heretical offenses" (Roth 99–100). But, as these offenses were necessarily secret, and therefore might not appear to be heretical at all, the edicts included detailed descriptions of the sorts of behaviors true Christians ought to look out for. Some of these behaviors constituted forms of religious observance which would, indeed, identify a practicing Jew, but others, like the smokeless chimneys on Saturdays, were not overt acts but merely absences or actions so commonplace that it was only in the Inquisitorial imagination that they could have significance at all. People were denounced for not eating hare, cuttlefish, or pork; for "putting on clean or festive clothes"; and for "cleaning their houses on Friday." Adherents to the Edicts of Faith were solemnly informed that Jews had a tendency to wash their hands (100–101), creating a social climate in which the "mere regard for personal cleanliness might be enough to convict a person of secretly practising Judaism . . . and so cost him his life" (105).[14]

I will return to the question of how late Victorian commentators on Shakespeare approached the Marrano Lopez and the matter of his relation to the figure of Shylock. But, before doing so, it will be helpful briefly to clarify several points of historiography.

The story of the Marranos is, as I have indicated, a traditional narrative that presents an epic of steadfast belief in the face of insuperable adversity, but, as Miriam Bodian has argued, the tendency to locate the problem of Marranism so firmly within the sphere of religion is reductive on several counts. The overemphasis on religion tends to discount questions of commercial and economic interest and to ignore the complexities of social and familial relationships and of self-perception and definition in a context in which people were subject to protracted and contradictory pressures. Thus, the Marranos are unified into a coherent group and the ineffable complexities of their Marranism reduced to a matter of religious fidelity or infidelity and, occasionally, even further to one of personal sincerity or insincerity.

Even more worrisome, however, is the extent to which the traditional account of the Marranos and their secret faith replicates the logic of Inquisitorial paranoia. For, although historians such as Cecil Roth embrace the cause of the Marranos, valorizing their crypto-Judaism, in order to do so they must leave intact the notion of the racial predisposition of Jews to duplicity. To put it another way, the concept of the Marranos' unshakable loyalty to Judaism is as tied as the tropes of the Inquisition are to the belief that Jewishness is a function of biology or of social characteristics so profoundly embedded that they are effectively quasi-biological. So, while these narratives champion rather than denounce the Marranos, they nevertheless participate in a discourse about Jews which attributes their social and political behavior to their race. More recent work has moved away from this presentation of crypto-Judaism as a coherent phenomenon.

Increasingly, for example, it has been recognized that "patterns of converso behaviour did not simply emerge from some primordial Jewish stratum of consciousness" and that Marrano identity, therefore, needs to be understood "as a changing cultural construction evolving over many generations and answering a variety of needs" (Bodian 50–51). Rather than secretly returning to Judaism at any cost, and with biologically programmed inevitability, Jewish converts to Catholicism displayed a wide range of responses to their respective situations, responses that varied tremendously, from generation to generation and from individual to individual, even among members of a single family. Moreover, compounding these differences were the relative levels of acceptance or rejection which Marranos experienced within their social and religious communities of resettlement and the variety of their relationships with the Jews and Gentiles they encountered outside the Iberian Peninsula. Most profoundly, however, as Yirmiyahu Yovel has argued:

> people do not discard their past simply because they
> make new decisions or embark upon a new course; a
> being endowed with consciousness and memory cannot

simply return to the point of departure, even when
reverting to a position once held in the past and then
abandoned. The Marranos had lived among Christians
for generations, partaken of their mores and education,
practised their customs—at least outwardly—and inter-
nalized the same symbolic universe and mode of thinking. (41)

Thus, whether they believed themselves to be true Christians,
Christians in name only, or once and forever Jews, the Marranos
clearly bore with them enduring confusions of identity which made
them, at best, the subjects of benign curiosity and, at worst, of op-
probrium and oppression. Only by recognizing these complexities
can we begin to appreciate the enduring fascination and treacherous
promise attached to figures such as Ruy Lopez and the Shylock he
may or may not have inspired.

I I I

The question of the Lopez affair and its relation to the figure of Shylock drew the attention of a number of critics and historians in the
latter decades of the nineteenth century.[15] These accounts portray
Lopez's treachery, his influence on the design of Shylock, and Shakespeare's intentions in representing the Jew. The study I would like to
focus on, however, is the one that addressed itself most directly to
the Victorian Shakespeare establishment and which was, most obviously, part of the wave of response to Irving's *Merchant of Venice*,
appearing as it did in the *Gentleman's Magazine* in February 1880,
about halfway through the production's opening run. Moreover, the
essay, entitled "The Original of Shylock," deserves particular notice
here not only for "attract[ing] . . . the attention of Shakespearean
scholars" (*SSL* 3) but also for its part in launching one of the Victorian era's most distinguished literary careers. The eighteen-year-old
undergraduate author of the essay went by the forenames Solomon
Lazarus. But, for the sake of his career he changed his name, it is
popularly believed, on the advice of Oxford's Benjamin Jowett, ironically, a man who had himself been accused of excessive displays of
religious radicalism.[16] As an eminent Shakespearean, editor of the

Dictionary of National Biography, first biographer of Queen Victoria, fellow of the British Academy, founding member of the English Association, and member of the Athenæum Club, to name only a few of his distinctions, Solomon Lazarus was better known to the world as Sidney or, more fully, as Sir Sidney Lee.

In his search for the original of Shylock, Sidney Lee posits four categories of evidence pertaining to the putative links between Shylock and his historical prototype. In outline he argues that the date of composition of *The Merchant of Venice* more or less coincides with the date of the alleged conspiracy and its aftermath; that the text of *The Merchant* contains topical references; that Shakespeare's protagonist, the merchant Antonio, was likely drawn with the protagonist of the Lopez affair in mind; and that Shylock and Lopez display similarities of character too great to be coincidental. As general categories of evidence, these seem fair enough, and, indeed, at the time of the article's publication they greatly impressed established authorities in Elizabethan studies such as J. O. Halliwell-Phillips and F. J. Furnivall. In the context of this study, however, the evidence that Sidney Lee offers with regard to Lopez and his relation to Shylock is compelling primarily in ways that the author and his contemporaries probably did not intend. Rather, what is remarkable from this vantage point is the extent to which the perception of a significant relation between the two figures is, effectively, inevitable, as are the particular narrative formulations mobilized in telling the story of Lopez and Shylock. It was a story that had been told before.

Sidney Lee's most straightforward argument is that pertaining to *The Merchant*'s date of composition, his claim being that the play "appeared for the first time not much more than three months after Lopez's famous execution" (Lee, "Original" 198). But, while it seems unlikely that Shakespeare—or, for that matter, anyone living in London at the time—would have been unaware of so public an event as the execution of the queen's personal physician, Lee's dating of the play and his connection of the two events is largely speculative. Nonetheless, at the time this would have constituted a scholarly argument. His remaining points, by way of contrast, display increasingly prominent elements of fantasy amid the learned speculation.

Lee's identification of topical references, for example, suggests that the connections he was arguing for were, in some imaginative sense, already in place. A conventional allusion to "the rack," which occurs as part of an exchange between the lovers Portia and Bassanio, is taken, without question, to allude to the fate of those implicated in the plot against Elizabeth,[17] while an anachronistic reference to trial by jury—a procedure not known in Venice during the time in which *The Merchant* is set—leads him directly to conclude that it must have been intended to suggest "the way in which an English court of law would treat a Jew" (Lee, "Original" 199). As far as the link between the protagonist of the play and the protagonist of the Lopez affair is concerned, somewhat fantastically, Lee's evidence here consists of little more than the fact that they were both called Antonio. Pointing out that "the name Antonio . . . was very common among the Portuguese"—the protagonist of the Lopez affair was Don Antonio, pretender to the Portuguese throne—it is not "by any means," Lee argues, "so ordinary an Italian one as Lorenzo or Ludovico" (197). It is difficult to know how to respond to this assertion, especially considering the stir it caused in the Shakespearean academic community at the time. To respond insofar as possible in the spirit of the author, however, one can only point out that, with the exception of certain "Citizens," "Servants," "Soldiers," "Ladies," "Gentlemen," and "Ghosts," Antonio is, as a matter of record, the single most commonly occurring name in all of Shakespeare's oeuvre.

Finally, there is Sidney Lee's claim that the similarities of character between Lopez and Shylock are too great to be coincidental. While Lee concedes that not much can be said definitively of Lopez's character, since his "extant correspondence is very incomplete, and gives us only glances here and there of his characteristics," he is nevertheless willing to comment, with authority, on points of character. Firstly, although he doesn't say why, Lee asserts "with some probability" that "the spirit of revenge in the doctor's case was similar in calibre to that in Shylock's." Even more to the point, however, he commits himself with "certainty" to the following claim:

> In their devotion to their family the two Jews closely
> resemble each other. Neither Lopez nor Shylock, in
> good fortune or in bad, fail to exemplify the Jewish

> virtue of domesticity. Lopez excused his attendance at
> court on the ground that the illness of his wife detained
> him at home. His Dutch correspondents never omit to
> send his family affectionate remembrances from his Jew-
> ish friends in Holland, whatever be the subject of the let-
> ter, and he never omits to return them. Similarly, Shy-
> lock's love for his daughter and for his wife Leah, whose
> memory he piously cherishes, are touches of character
> which theories of dramatic art only incompletely explain.
> (Lee, "Original" 198–99)

There are two chronically recurring narratives at work here, the first
of which is the story of "the Jewish virtue of domesticity," a virtue
that, as we have already seen, necessarily connotes hidden vice. The
fact that Lopez's correspondence includes conventional greetings and
inquiries after the welfare of friends abroad or that, as a husband and
doctor, he should have attended his wife in illness is to Sidney Lee, as
they would undoubtedly have been to the Inquisition, signs of the
innately suspect nature of Jews. Here, as everywhere else, Jewish participation in the commonplace is a sign of secret goings-on. Thus,
the fact that Shylock loves his daughter and reveres the memory of
his dead wife cannot possibly be taken at face value. They are enig-
matic signifiers, "touches of character which theories of dramatic art
only incompletely explain."

The second narrative at work here is one that Sidney Lee authored but did not, in any ordinary sense, write. For, like a man
holding up a mirror while looking in the mirror, Sidney Lee, in
rooting out the story of Lopez embedded in the figure of Shylock,
manifested yet again the infinitely regressive life of the secret Jew.
The story of Lee's own life is the story of a great public figure, a man
who made his way, by virtue of his talent and industry, to the top
of the Victorian intellectual establishment; it is the story of a man
deemed fit to write the life of the queen. Considering the accomplishments he could list by the time he died, one would hardly remember that what had launched his career was nothing more than
an essay exposing the relation of an infamous Jewish villain to a
secret Jew, a great public figure who, like Lee himself, had made

his way, by virtue of his talent and industry, to the top of the Elizabethan establishment and who, until he was found out, had been
deemed fit to guard the life of the queen. Even less would it be re-
membered that until he had written that essay, as a young man, Sir
Sidney had gone by another name.

4 "Which Is the Merchant Here? And Which the Jew?"

Not very far from the city of Verona in Italy, is another city that is the most wonderful and beautiful town in Europe, and perhaps in all the world. It is called Venice . . . The people who made this city long ago were very fond of beautiful things, and as there were no railways or telegraphs, or steam-boats, in those days there was not so much hurry and scurry, and they had plenty of time to build their houses and ornament them, so they got many coloured marbles and carved the stone that they used; and instead of having long lines of houses, with two windows and a door and ugly areas, all so alike, that we have to put numbers on them so as to know which is the one we live in, every rich man built his house just as he chose . . . Now, as this city of Venice is quite on the sea, in olden times the Venetians had a great many ships that they used to send to foreign countries, to fetch silks and spices, and diamonds and pearls, and gold and silver, and all kinds of things, which come from India and other far-off places; and then they sold these precious goods to people in France, and England, and Germany; and made a great deal of money, and spent it in making their city of Venice more and more beautiful.

These men were called merchants, and one of the greatest of them was an old man named Antonio. Antonio had neither wife nor children, but spent his money in kind charitable ways, and in helping to build splendid churches and palaces in the city. Everyone who was in trouble came to him for help and advice . . . There was [also] an old Jew in Venice, called Shylock, who was richer than any of the merchants, because he never spent more of his money than he could help, but hoarded it up, and saved it; and sometimes, when other people were hard up, he would lend them a little; but on condition that when they paid him back they should always give him more than he had lent them . . . and so he grew very rich. But, as he was mean and hard, the people in Venice hated him, and he knew it, and hated them even more; and he was always glad when he could screw money out of a poor Christian, who wanted a little help; for you know there was always a quarrel between the Jews and the Christians, because it was the Jews crucified our Saviour, whom the Christians know was the Son of God; and for many years they could not forgive the Jews, and would not treat them like fellow countrymen, but rather like slaves. (Gordon 80–85)

In the deep blue sea of the Adriatic lies the wonderful city of Venice. It is built on a hundred and seventeen small islands . . . Beautiful marble palaces are built on some of the islands . . . wonderful churches and galleries, full of the finest pictures and art-treasures, are on others; and gardens, markets, squares, and shops, with smaller houses for poor people, are found clustering together elsewhere. Instead of carriages and carts the Venetians use long, narrow boats called gondolas, which, since Venice ceased to be a powerful Republic . . . have always been painted black in token of mourning.

But years ago . . . when the story you now read took place, Venice was at the height of her glory and power, and from this sea-girt city sailed forth wonderful ships . . . loaded with all the riches and treasures of the then known world, for Venice was the great trading centre for all parts; and on the famous Rialto, the island devoted to the business of the city, met all the wealthy merchants of Venice and traders from everywhere, East and West.

Amongst the flowing mantles of rich brocade worn by the Venetians might be seen the long sober gabardines of the Jews, a people at that time much hated and despised, but who, notwithstanding the unjust persecution they suffered for their religion, managed to enrich themselves, and, because of their riches, became a power in any State who would let them live in tolerable security in the land. It is not much to be wondered at that the Jews returned the hatred with interest, and that when occasion offered they drove as hard a bargain, or got the better of any Gentile, as was possible. Hate breeds hate, and the Christians showed as little of their Master's spirit as did the Jews, who denied Him.

The market-place was surrounded by colonnades, with fine paintings on the walls, and there also hung a large map, showing the route of the Venetian merchant ships all over the world. At one corner stood a church, the oldest in Venice, and on its wall was this inscription:

"Around this temple let the merchant's law be just, his weight true, and his covenant faithful."

For such was the standard set before the Venetian people; and that their laws were good and true for friend or alien was one of their proud boasts. (Maud and Maud 267–70)

These excerpts present just two of the seemingly innumerable versions of *The Merchant of Venice* which constituted a prominent and influential category of texts about the text in the late nineteenth and early twentieth centuries. These were reworkings of *The Merchant* narrative intended for educational purposes, most often to be read by children.[1] Didactic versions of Shakespeare plays generally took one of several forms at the time. They were either renditions, like the widely acclaimed Lamb's *Tales* or the ones reproduced here; or they were school editions of the plays which could be either pamphlet-style extracts or complete texts accompanied by commentaries, notes for study, and questions for examination.

To locate these texts historically, they are part of the boom in juvenile publishing which began in the 1860s and reached its height in the period between 1880 and 1910.[2] It was in this period that the belief that had hitherto dominated the production of children's books—namely, that they should, by definition, be morally instructive—gave way to a growing sense of the legitimacy of the idea of literary pleasures for children. This was also the period following the 1870 Education Act and the expansion of the public library system, both of which formalized the new social commitment to compulsory education and, hence, literacy, at least in principle, for all children. Moreover, rapidly improving publishing technologies made it possible both for ordinary school texts and for ornate and beautifully illustrated books to be produced and sold at a fraction of previous costs.[3] To give some indication of the scale of production of children's versions of Shakespeare, over sixty school editions of *The Merchant of Venice* alone were published between 1870 and 1920.[4] And, while Charles and Mary Lamb's celebrated *Tales* (1807) spawned no imitators for nearly three quarters of a century, the 1880s marked the beginning of a spate of Shakespeare's tales retold and illustrated for children.[5]

These texts have obvious significance, then, as part of an important social trend. From the 1860s onward "those who wrote books for children were in a more assured social position than ever before. They were more nearly of the 'ruling' classes . . . [and] had a modest feeling of prerogative audiences" (Darton 252). The books they produced thus reflect a shift away from evangelical and conservative values toward increasingly liberal and secular ones. If there were evil in the world, the new mandate of children's literature was not to participate in the duty of child surveillance but, rather, "to combat evil by treating goodness as ordinary unemphasized decency and honesty, which knew and avoided vice spontaneously, and rejected it . . . with vigour, but without loud chords of moral triumph" (299).

But it is not simply because there were a lot of these texts around or even that they exemplify certain liberal attitudes toward juvenile publishing in Victorian society that they are of interest here. Nor will this chapter be primarily concerned with their rather obvious moralizing and chauvinistic agenda. Indeed, in a sense my interest in them is not directly tied to their status as children's literature per se but, instead, to the ways in which they mobilize the territorial imperatives both of the sphere of literature and of the realm of childhood. For, as Jacqueline Rose has argued, literature, and especially children's literature, is seen to be the "repository of a privileged experience and sensibility at risk in the outside world where . . . values are being crushed under the weight of cultural decay" and which, therefore, holds out the promise of "prolonging or preserving—not only for the child but also for us—values which are constantly on the verge of collapse" (Rose 43–44). Thus, my interest here is not in what adults were demanding of the children for whom they wrote these texts but, rather, in the ways in which these children's versions of Shakespeare provided, *for adults,* a quasi-sacred territory of retreat in which disturbing changes in society could, at least momentarily, be banished, ignored, or innocently overcome.

I

While the two versions of the story are similar in ways that allow us to derive the dominant form that juvenile discourses about *The Merchant* tended to take, what is equally, if not ultimately, more important here are the differences between them which identify these texts as a site of intensely competing interests. To put it another way, despite the powerful uniformities of tone across these texts which may encourage us to read them primarily as signs of late Victorian bourgeois hegemony, by no means was there consensus either about the precise form the story should take or about its ultimate meaning. I will come to these differences in a moment, but first it will be helpful to consider the similarities between the two narratives in order to draw a fuller picture of the dominant discourse in which they both participate.

Three tropes, or figures, common to the two narratives appear to be common to most late-nineteenth- and early-twentieth-century juvenile renditions of *The Merchant of Venice.* First, there is the city of Venice as great mercantile capital and enchanted place. Second, there are the merchants, who are the first citizens of Venice. And, third, there are the Jews, who figure as a dark presence both within the enchanted city and the community of merchants. I shall elaborate on each of these in turn.

Venice is an enchanted place, a city of light and indescribable beauty where every house is a palace because here ornament overrules function, and every stone is a monument to individualism harnessed in the service of society. If there are any poor people in Venice, their homes are small but picturesque, and they meld easily into the liveliness of the crowded squares and the abundance of the marketplace. There is no ugliness, no poverty, no industrialization. This is the city free from the ills of modernity; Venice is a place where people walk on water. Moreover, Venice is a great mercantile capital, a place from whence ships set sail to all parts of the world and to which they return laden with precious and wonderful things. The merchants sell these things to people in other places, and so they become very rich, and Venice becomes more enchanted and more enchanting than ever. Venice is a city that changes only by becoming more beautiful.

The people of Venice are all merchants, or at least they are the ones we can see and who clearly matter. These are the men who own the ships, who build the palaces, and who make the city beautiful. They wear magnificent robes so we can easily tell who they are.

Finally, there are the Jews, the one cloud that hangs over the city of Venice. The Jews are also merchants but not of the usual kind. They do not wear brocades or live in palaces, even though they too are very rich. Unlike the other merchants, the Jews appear to have gotten rich not by trading in magnificence but by preying on those who have fallen on hard times. They do this because they hate Christians. Christians hate them back.

It is not difficult to see that, whatever else they may be, these are stories about empire before the Fall, Venice in its dual role as city and state standing in, at once, for the British Empire and for London, its enchanted mercantile capital. For, in much the same way that Victorians looked to imperial Rome as an analogue of their own rise and fall, they mythologized Venice as a great republic. Immortalized by the likes of Ruskin and Turner, Venice was, for late Victorian society,

"all wonder, enchantment . . . brightness and the glory of a dream"
(Oliphant 2). Unlike the cities of England or, for that matter, anywhere else, it was a place where "great palaces, solid and splendid,
[were] built, so to speak, on nothing" and where the "harsh, artificial
sounds which vex the air in other towns" were "replaced by har-
monies of human voices, and by the liquid tinkle of the waves" (1).
Even beyond its peerless beauty the city's virtues were legion. Venice
was

> a power which was once supreme in the seas, the arbiter
> of peace and war through all the difficult and dangerous
> East, the first defender of Christendom against the Turk,
> the first merchant, banker, carrier whose emissaries were
> busy in all the councils and all the markets of the world
> . . . the worshipped ideal of a community in which every
> man for the common glory seems to have been willing
> to sink his own. Her sons toiled for her, each in his voca-
> tion, not without personal glory, far from indifferent to
> personal gain, yet determined above all that Venice
> should be great, that she should be beautiful above all
> the thoughts of other races, that her power and her
> splendour should outdo every rival. (3–4)

In short, Venice at the height of its glory and power was what the
British Empire longed to be, and no opportunity was lost in instill-
ing this longing in students of Shakespeare. Through Shakespeare's
image of Venice they were reassured:

> we are impressed with the dignity of a municipality,
> proud of its charters and its freedom; we can almost real-
> ize the unrivalled blue of its skies, and hear the dip of the
> oars in its famous canals; we feel that the poet has ethe-
> realized the whole, and has made Venice an eternal city,
> a city which will survive "The wreck of matter and the
> crash of worlds." (Barnett 12–13)

Clearly, this idealization of Venice was meant, broadly speaking,
to compensate for the less than ideal circumstances of late imperial
and industrial society in Britain. But with reference to Shakespeare's

play the mythologizing seemed to take on an added dimension. For, while the constraints of polite society might have deterred late Victorian subjects from making direct comparisons between the first earthly Paradise and their own green and pleasant land, they were manifestly at ease with a narrative about capital, nation, and empire in which Venice stood in, syllogistically, for England on the one hand and for the Garden of Eden on the other. Because it overlaid a long-standing myth of empire with a tale of mercenary commerce which was, at yet another level, a parable about the respective moralities of Christians and Jews, *The Merchant of Venice* seemed not simply to endorse the widely held belief in Shakespeare as secular scripture but, indeed, to announce itself as an ersatz Book of Genesis, as the myth of creation rewritten to address the needs of Victorian capitalism in troubled times.

The advantages of such a myth were clear. Like all typological tales, it rationalized the present by predicating it in a sacred past linked to a redemptive future. Thus, within its frame of reference the social costs of industrialization and the increasing uncertainties of empire could be read not as the consequences of historical acts willfully undertaken but, rather, as the divinely inspired trials endured by men as a function of their humanity and as a prelude to their salvation. Moreover, since the myth depends on Venice's dual status as both a manifestation of Paradise on earth and as the legendary home of venture capital, it allows the merchants, the first citizens of Venice, to assume a vital symbolic role. For, if Venice figures the Garden of Eden, then the merchant is recast as the father of humanity; the Victorian capitalist becomes primordial man.

At one level the myth functions beautifully—what could be more compelling than a typological reading of Victorian capitalism? But at another level it leads to something of an impasse. The problem is this: if *The Merchant of Venice* is the story of Victorian capitalism recast as the myth of creation, then where do we locate Shylock? Surely, both ancient right and infamous modern reputation would suggest that, if anyone in this story were going to get to be primordial man, it ought to be the Jew. But installing an aggrieved and vocal Jew as the father of humanity was clearly not the point of the exercise. And, if we return now to our two extracts and, more specifically, to the differences between them, we can begin to get a more detailed sense of the problem and the variety of ways in which it was handled.

We can think about the differences between the two texts in a number of ways. We can see, for example, that the two texts display very different senses of history. In the first extract the past is unequivocally sentimental; history is little more than the bygone era of "once-upon-a-time," and the distance between past and present is easily traversed by cheerful references to "the people who made this city long ago" and who ventured forth from its shores "in olden times." There is nothing to indicate that the present is, in any way, unlike that idealized past, as we are offered up an unadulterated vision of empire in its enduring splendor and glory. In the second extract history is significantly more consequential. We can sense this partly from the comparatively reserved tone of the piece and partly from the clear distinction it makes between the present and the time "years ago . . . when the story you now read took place." Mostly, however, its more considered sense of history is conveyed by the arresting detail of the gondolas, "which, since Venice ceased to be a powerful Republic . . . have always been painted black in token of mourning." Correspondingly, while the first text is resolutely antimodern, reveling, as it does, in the absence of ugliness, railways, and telegraphs, for the second carriages, carts, and the small houses of the poor are simply facts of life. The most telling differences between the two narratives, however, have to do with the ways in which they rationalize the presence of Jews within the mythical republic. For it is the presence of Jews more than any single element in these texts which seems to signal the crisis of modernity, the expulsion from Paradise, and the inevitable Fall.

The first narrative is a classic typological tale. The Jews are, without a doubt, the Jews of typological antiquity, the outsiders whose perversity and "obdurate blindness" have led them to deny the divinity of Christ (Auerbach, "Figura" 40), a sin that they habitually reenact by "screwing money out of . . . poor Christian[s]." They are mean and hard and quarrelsome and thus the authors of their own misfortune and the sole agents of their perpetually marginalized existence. Their status as citizens within the republic is irrevocably linked to their typological role; the "fact" that they "crucified our Saviour" separates them absolutely from their Christian counterparts and determines that they will forever be treated "not like fellow countrymen, but rather like slaves." There is no secularism here. The glorious vision of empire is, at one and the same time, a celebration of Christianity. Thus, the eventual defeat of Shylock in a court of law proclaims not just the integrity of the republic and the triumph of virtuous citizens over diabolic outsiders but, equally, the triumph of believers over nonbelievers, of the Gospels over the Old Testament, of Christians over Jews.

In the second of our two narratives the situation is rather more complex. The splendor of the republic has faded, there is a marked separation of church and state, and the doctrinal certainties of Christianity have given way to the ambiguities of liberalism. While there is recognition of the fact that the persecution of the Jews has been "unjust," that "the Christians showed as little of their Master's spirit as did the Jews, who denied Him," and that "Hate breeds hate," there is equally the familiar sense of begrudging unease with a people who, "notwithstanding the unjust persecution they suffered . . . managed to enrich themselves, and, because of their riches, became a power in any State who would let them live with tolerable security in the land." Clearly, in the context of this second narrative it will take more than a myth of Venice as an earthly Paradise to secure the integrity of the state. The wealth of the republic and the viability of its imperial aspirations cannot, in this case, stand for the richness of its morality. Rather, the investment here is in the rule of law: "Let the merchant's law be just, his weight true, and his covenant faithful." The state has staked a new claim for its integrity, and the Jew is central to all this, for, if his marginal status is no longer attributable to his contempt for Christ, then it must now be accounted for in some other way. And, if the state is indeed committed to the ideal that "its laws were good and true for friend or alien," then it is the Jew in the story who puts this claim to the test.

The fact that nearly two decades elapsed between the publication of the two texts prompts us to ask whether the differences between them can be understood chronologically, in terms of an obvious development or series of events which occurred between 1894 and 1913.

We may wonder, for instance, whether the greater liberalism and secularism of the latter text corresponds with a clear shift, say, in public attitudes toward Jews in England over that time. While this may, in some very general way, be true, what I will argue is that, with reference to these texts, in no simple sense is this the case. Read against the background of the historical debate that best illuminates this discussion, what we see is not a progression from one position to the next but, rather, the simultaneity of the two. What I am arguing, in other words, is that these two versions of the story of the Jewish capitalist in Christian society exist side by side, in perpetual conflict, and without any obvious resolution. The historical debate that provides the background here is the debate over usury, a debate of ancient provenance which was taken up with renewed urgency in England in the nineteenth century but, ultimately, remained unresolved.

I I

In his preface to an edition of *The Merchant of Venice* "abbreviated and adapted for social reading in parts," John Earle, of "the Swanswick Shakespeare Society, of limited liability," observed the following:

> In our day the right to receive interest is no more
> doubted than the right to receive rent. But how
> lately this opinion has been matured [and] by what
> circuitous fictions, and cunning expediencies, men
> eluded a religious obligation which they ought rather
> to have disputed, would fill an essay, and a curious
> one it would be. (vi)

The religious obligation to which Earle refers is, of course, the biblical injunction against usury, an injunction that, although enduringly effective in ostracizing Jews, had caused perennial inconvenience to honest businessmen like Antonio and other "merchant-princes" and "gentlemen of chivalrous and punctilious honour" from biblical times to the present. As Earle saw it, the fatal flaw in the concept of usury, especially as it was passed into English law during the reign of Edward VI, was that the "censure is directed, not against lending money *on hard terms,* such as we should now call usurious; but simply against the practice, *whatever the terms,* of lending money on interest" (vi–vii; my emph.). Hence, Earle's remarks about the "circuitous fictions" and "cunning expediencies" that the apologists of commerce had to resort to—in times less enlightened than his own—in order to bypass the biblical injunction without forfeiting their moral superiority over the Jews.[6] The point is, of course, that to John Earle such fictions seemed unnecessary, because, as any schoolchild who had ever studied Shakespeare could tell you, no one could possibly mistake an honest merchant for a usurious Jew. Or maybe one could.

The immorality of taking money for the loan of money versus the need for unobstructed access to capital—in effect, the question of morality versus the public convenience—has been debated at least from the time of Aristotle onward and is by no means confined to European societies or linked in any simple or deterministic sense to questions of anti-Semitism and the history of European Jews. Indeed, the legendary association of Jews with usurious practice has tended to obscure the extent to which debates about usury are not exclusively moral but, rather, engage complex economic, social, and political factors in determining whether the church or the state will control access to, and attitudes governing, money and the acquisition of wealth and, secondarily, the extent to which the church or state should intervene in the workings of the economy at all. We can see this in a Victorian context, in which religious arguments against usury were increasingly marginalized by the demands of the financial sector, the economic concerns of secular government, and the discourses of political economy.[7]

The reemergence of the debate in nineteenth-century England crystallized around a critique of the concept of usury mounted, most famously, by Jeremy Bentham in his essay "Defence of Usury" (1787) but which was sustained equally by David Hume and Adam Smith (Bellot and Willis 29). The terms of the critique were the now familiar ones—namely, that "the rate of interest would, if left alone, settle itself according to the laws of political economy, and that legislative restraints were not only useless but actually pernicious" (vii). Furthermore, as Bentham argued, nobody really knew what usury was, since no positive definition of the term had ever existed. Rather, there were two competing negative definitions, one legal, the other moral. The former defined usury as "the taking of more interest than the law allows," while the latter defined it as "the taking of more interest than it is usual for men to give and take" (Bentham 4). The problem with the moral definition—crucial because, in the absence of anti-usury legislation, it was the one that prevailed—was that interest rates were fixed by nothing more than a highly localized sense of custom and vague notions of necessity and luxury. The problems with the legal definition of usury were legion.

In order for a legal definition of usury to stand, a clear, positive description of the practice was required. In short, a better definition had to be arrived at than one that named usury simply as the opposite of conventionally moral or legal practice with regard to money-lending. In the absence of such a definition no legal rate of interest could ever be set, usury prevented, or usurers legally known. As we shall see, from a legislative standpoint this problem was never really solved. But beyond this considerable obstacle other problems remained.

Why, for example, Bentham asked, should legislators single out interest rates for legislative intervention?

> For him who takes as much as he can get for the use of any other sort of thing, a house, for instance, there is no particular appellation, nor any mark of disrepute . . . Why a man who takes as much as he can get . . . for the use of a sum of money, should be called usurer, should be loaded with an opprobrious name, any more than if he had bought a house with it, and made a proportion-able profit . . . is more than I can see. (4)

Moreover, if a legal rate of interest were going to be set, why not penalize those who loan money out at rates lower than the designated level as well as those who exceed it? (4–5). The justifications commonly cited in support of anti-usury legislation—prevention of prodigality and protection of indigence, for instance—were paternalistic, unlikely to prevent these things from happening in any case, and were more than likely to worsen rather than improve the situations of people in need of loans (5–8). Besides, there were scores of ways in which anti-usury legislation could be evaded; commissions, annuities, trading in bills of sale, pawnbroking, and insurance could all be used to alter the rate at which money was loaned. How, then, could such legislation ever be enforceable, particularly when legitimate, solvent businessmen were prevented from deciding for themselves what they could or should do to capitalize their trade?

On the strength of arguments such as these a Parliamentary Select Committee was appointed in 1818 "to consider the effects of the Laws which regulate or restrain the Interest of Money."[8] Composed largely of men with a manifest interest in seeing the usury laws repealed—Nehemiah Rothschild and David Ricardo, for example—not surprisingly, the committee agreed to a set of resolutions very much in line with the arguments of the political economists. They found that

> the Laws regulating . . . the rate of Interest have been extensively evaded . . . [and] that the constant excess of the market rate of interest above the rate limited by law . . . [has] added to the expense incurred by borrowers on real security . . . and has further subjected borrowers to enormous charges, or forced them to make very disadvantageous sales of their estates. (PP 1818, 141)

Furthermore, the committee found, the existing laws left people constantly in doubt about the legality of their transactions, resulting in "much embarrassment and litigation." Hence, they called for the complete abolition of all anti-usury legislation.

Despite the findings of the committee, however, no direct or comprehensive legislative action was undertaken. Rather, over a number of years various amendments were made which whittled away at the problem, until all the existing anti-usury legislation was finally repealed in 1854.[9] But the problem was by no means resolved, for by the 1890s there was so great a demand for the laws to be reinstated that in 1897 another parliamentary committee was appointed.[10] This time an important distinction that had been ignored in 1818—namely, one differentiating middle-class borrowers from the needy and desperate—was brought to the fore.[11] And, unlike the committee of

1818, which had lent its ear to political economists and venture capitalists, the committee of 1897 called before it moneylenders and their hapless victims, and expert testimony came not from men with an overwhelming interest in business but from judges who presided over prosecutions involving moneylenders and their debtors and from those committed to exposing the evil of usury. At times the evidence conjured up scenes worthy of Victorian melodrama.

Perhaps the single most important witness to come before the committee was Thomas Farrow, a banker by profession, self-appointed crusader against usury, and author of several popular works, including *The Money-lender Unmasked* (1895) and *In the Money-lender's Clutches* (1896).[12] In these works, as in his testimony before the committee, Farrow detailed the methods by which moneylenders lured unsuspecting and often desperate borrowers into their reach.

Misleading advertisements were placed in newspapers offering ready cash and complete confidentiality to anyone in need of a loan. Typically, what the ads failed to mention was that substantial, non-refundable fees were charged for the mere processing of applications so that the moneylender was bound to profit even if he ultimately decided not to lend anything at all. Moreover, there existed an information network, known colloquially as the "Secret Circle" (PP 1897, 420), which was served by a publication called *Perry's Gazette*. The Secret Circle traded in confidential information about prospective borrowers; moneylenders subscribing to this service could thus easily determine the extent to which borrowers were already indebted and could, therefore, more easily calculate the level of risk that lending to them entailed.

Once a borrower had been deemed an acceptable risk, a lending agreement was signed. According to Farrow, the documents were frequently folded in such a way that borrowers were prevented from seeing what they were signing, or else the relevant clauses were obscured with blotting paper. He also testified that it was common practice for moneylenders to add the words *per month* to the contract after it was signed, thus altering the rate of interest from 5 percent to 5 percent per month, or 60 percent per annum. Alternately, he reported, the letters *ty* were sometimes added after the word *six* to similar effect (PP 1897, 421). Moneylenders were also under no obligation to register themselves or their businesses or to trade under their own names. Consequently, some borrowers who attempted to protect their meager assets by taking out a number of small loans with two or three different moneylenders eventually found themselves under obligation two or three times over to a single man trading under multiple aliases (432–33).

Some of the recommendations arising from the committee's investigations—forbidding moneylenders to refer to themselves as banks and making it illegal to trade under more than one name, for example—could easily be translated into legislation. But the fundamental problem, that of legally defining usury, remained. This fact is particularly evident in the testimony of Judge William Stevenson Owen, a county court judge in Cardiff. In his testimony Owen had stressed that, unless a legal definition of usury could be arrived at, the problem could never be dealt with effectively (PP 1897, 623). Thus, he was charged with the responsibility of devising such a definition and submitting it to the committee. While Owen said that he was happy to undertake the task, he was equally aware that "whoever has to draft any legislation following the Committee's report . . . will have a very tough job" (624). Owen's instincts were right, as his letter to the chairman of the committee shows:

> Ty Gwyn, Abergavenny, 24 July 1897
>
> Sir,
>
> When I had the honour of giving evidence before your Committee, On Tuesday last, you asked me to send you, if I were able to do so, a definition of the words "moneylender," or "moneylending."
>
> I am sorry to say that I have failed to give a definition which would be sufficient, and exhaustive. You will, probably, agree with me in thinking that a definition which does not cover every case would be worse than useless.

Owen goes on to say that, unlike hawkers, peddlers, pawnbrokers, and bankers, all of whom had been adequately defined for the purpose of drafting legislation, the case of moneylenders had proved intractable. Moreover, because moneylending had proved such a

slippery business, Owen warned that, "even if a satisfactory definition of 'moneylender' can be given, it would not be advisable in
any Act which may result from the Report of your Committee, to
attempt to give a definition." Rather, he proposed a compromise
wherein new legislation would contain the following clause:

> No person, partnership, or company who exercise or
> carry on the trade or business of money lending shall be
> entitled to recover in any court of law any money lent or
> any interest, commission, reward, fee, fine, expenses,
> profit or other payments whatsoever in respect of any
> money lent or in respect of any application to offer or
> lend or borrow money unless duly registered and
> licensed as provided by this Act. (695)

But all this meant was that no unregistered moneylender could pursue a suit in court against a defaulting borrower; it did not force
moneylenders to register nor prevent unregistered lenders from car-
rying on as they liked. Neither would such a clause prevent the collection of fees for application, the trade in confidential information,
or the collection of repayments before the borrower fell into arrears.
In short the inclusion of such a clause in future legislation could do
little more than remove the need for judges to have to determine
the status of plaintiffs on a case-by-case basis. If someone were regis-
tered as a moneylender, he was a moneylender; otherwise, he was
not. In sum, there was little the law could do to guard against a
practice that no one, not even the experts, could define.

In 1899 a bill was introduced into the House of Lords, but, because
it was introduced so late in the session, it failed to become law. Re-
introduced the following year, this bill became the Money-Lenders
Act of 1900 (H. Reed 15).

What is key about the Money-Lenders Act, in terms of this discussion, is the way in which it signaled a shift away from the attempt to
deal with usury by determining a legal rate of interest, toward an
emphasis on identifying and defining what came to be known as
"the unconscionable bargain."[13] As the legal expert Haythorne Reed
indicated, on the subject of moneylending legal opinion had finally
given way to political economy:

> Interest is the equivalent for two things—it is a charge
> for the use of the money lent and for the risk of losing it.
>   As the rate of interest, therefore, must depend on such
> variable circumstances as the state of the market and the
> nature of the security offered, no maximum can be safely
> laid down above which interest is to be deemed exces-
> sive; and it is obvious that what is a fair interest when
> the borrower is a substantial man, the security good, and
> the bank rate low, must differ so much from what is a
> fair interest when the borrower is a man who can give
> no security, and who has no character to lose, and the
> bank rate very high that any fixed scale can be a reliable
> guide. (29)

Crucially, what this meant was that, from a legal standpoint, there
could be no assumed relation between the level of interest charged
and the essential nature of the contract—in effect, "no . . . arbitrary
deduction that because a high rate of interest is charged, the bargain
is harsh and unconscionable" (30). Defining the unconscionable bargain involved a number of considerations, including "the relations
in which the parties stand to one another," "the rate of interest
charged upon the loan," and "the character of the security given or
promised" (31). If "the weaker party had no legal or independent
advice" (36), if they were "uneducated or ignorant" (37) or had been
tricked or pressured into the contract (38–39), the deal could be
deemed unconscionable and therefore liable to legal intervention.
But there were so many possible variables that no clear set of rules
could be drafted. Whether a bargain was unconscionable or not was
a matter to be decided by the court with "regard . . . to the circumstances of each particular case" (31).
    After nearly a century of renewed investigation and debate, all that
had happened was that Parliament had once again—and this time
quite spectacularly—begged the question. A usurer, then, was anyone so named by the law. Honest businessmen could, presumably,
rest easy, regardless of the rate of interest they charged, while evil
tricksters should not expect to profit from their day in court. And,
although centuries of debate had demonstrated that nobody could
really tell the two figures apart, the Money-Lenders Act said that

smart money was on the wise judges. Surely, they would see these people for who they were.

I I I

That *The Merchant of Venice* set the standard for commercial conduct in late Victorian society was a point commonly made by commentators on the text. C. H. Herford argued that, since

> almost every one in the play is in some way brought into relation with the getting, or keeping, or spending, or losing of wealth . . . one might say that the touchstone by which each character is tried is the attitude towards wealth which he assumes. (72)

Likewise, Stanley Wood noticed that in *The Merchant of Venice* "Shakespeare has enabled us to see the different effects upon different characters of the possession of wealth" (Supplement 6–7). Thus, in order to distinguish good from bad one had only to "contrast the character of Antonio with that of Shylock, referring . . . particularly to their respective attitudes with regard to wealth and the use of money" (11). In countless school editions of *The Merchant of Venice* this distinction was elaborately inscribed.

"A more perfect contrast to the Jew," wrote Wood, "could not have been framed than the merchant Antonio":

> He is also rich, but his heart has not been set upon his riches. He employs his wealth only for the benefit of others; his pleasure in it is in exact proportion to the enjoyment he can give to others by its means . . . his house is open to all his acquaintances and he not only puts all his money at the disposal of his friend [Bassanio] but places his life in peril for his sake. Unlike the crooked shuffling Jew, Antonio is candid and unsuspicious, untouched by trivial anxieties, indifferent to worldly ambitions, incautious, careless, generous. (Supplement 12)

Similarly, C. W. Crook maintained that, being "ready and eager to put all his resources at his friend's disposal," Antonio "resents even the hesitation which Bassanio shows in asking":

> Although unable from his own resources to provide the money needed by Bassanio, he readily urges Bassanio to pledge his credit, and cheerfully accepts the bond which Shylock proposes . . . When misfortune after misfortune prevents the meeting of the bond . . . he prepares to meet his fate with a calm resignation, happy to have his friend Bassanio at his side, and happy still to pay his friend's debt with his own life. (xlviii)

"Gentle, generous, [and] magnanimous" (Leppington 74), "sanguine [and] enthusiastic," possessed of a "high-soaring mind" (Earle x), and utterly "indifferent to wealth" (Wood, Supplement 7), Antonio invoked comparisons with some of the greatest men who had ever lived. "Just as it is impossible to read The Tempest without identifying Shakespeare . . . with Prospero," wrote T. Duff Barnett, so we cannot help looking on Antonio as a pale reflex of the poet himself" (7). And, taking the comparison one step nearer its logical conclusion, John Earle declared Antonio to be an "isolated mortal" whose manifest "superiority" left him "lonely in a crowd, like Adam in the midst of the cattle" (x).

We can see, then, what an extraordinary figure the good capitalist, epitomized by the figure of Antonio, cut. His wealth was largely incidental, accrued by unspecified means and probably by accident. He never counted it, talked about it, or spent it on himself. In fact, the good capitalist was prone to give his money away—all of it, at every possible opportunity, and apparently at no cost to himself. Being vital to existence but not, strictly speaking, a possession, money passed through the good capitalist's hands in much the same way that water passed through his lips and air moved through his lungs. To the good capitalist profit was as nothing when compared with honor, a principle he regularly defended by offering up his life as security for the business ventures of his friends. In sum the good capitalist was easy to spot because he was the one not in it for the money.

But, while some people's financial acumen was thus reworked into an elaborate system of signs in which the construct "good capitalist" always also signified "good Christian," "good citizen," "good husband," "good father," "good gentlemen," "good leader," "good friend," the signs did not always line up as they should. We can see this very clearly if we take the case of the unfortunate Bassanio. For, being of noble origins but severely hampered by a cash-flow problem and a checkered past, Bassanio was the character who, more than any other, seemed to test the mental agility of those whose job it was to ensure that the good characters in *The Merchant of Venice* were clearly distinguishable from the bad.

The preferred line of attack in the struggle to secure Bassanio's rightful designation was the time-honored one of blaming his evident shortcomings on the faulty perceptions of the reader. "To a casual observer," wrote Stanley Wood, "Bassanio appears to be an inconsiderate and selfish character, but careless and extravagant though he appears, there was, nevertheless, that within him which justified Antonio's deep affection for him" (Manuals 11):

> Bassanio is a character, with regard to whom a merely superficial view is likely to create a false impression in the mind of the reader. There is about him an air of selfishness, wildness, and self-seeking. But the love which Antonio and Portia . . . felt towards him, sets upon him, as it were, the seal of merit; it behoves us, therefore, to seek to discover in him qualities which render him worthy of such high favour. (Supplement 16)

"The deference shown to him by the other characters in the play, and the natural manner in which he assumes the leading place in the company of his friends, show that extravagance"—the tragic flaw of good capitalists—"was the greatest fault which could be laid to [Bassanio's] charge" (Crook lii). Besides, Bassanio repented, and, like all those who have strayed from the path of virtue, his return to the fold was especially prized. While "in his youth he had been prodigal of substance, 'his hours fill'd up with riots, banquets, sports,'" Bassanio "has seen the error of his ways" and is "anxious 'to come fairly off' from his great debts" (Wood, Supplement 16). The fact that he declares his intention to do so by means of gold digging is of no consequence, for there are established precedents for the move:

> Bassanio is the type of the well-born and well-educated
> young man who attempts to repair the ravages of an
> extravagant youth by a wealthy marriage. He does this,
> however, under no false pretences . . . and the seeking in
> marriage of a rich heiress was then, as now, by no means
> an unusual or despised resource of the noble born.
> (Crook li)

Noblemen appearing to fall short of the mark only appear that way
to those who cannot see below the surface of things. "The circle in
which Antonio is the most conspicuous figure is marked by a lordly
prodigality," and of all Portia's suitors only Bassanio eschewed the
"lust of splendour" and chose the lead casket by seeing with his noble
heart and not his common eyes (Herford 72). The simple fact that
figures as highly rated as Portia and Antonio choose Bassanio as the
object of their affections finds him "innocent by association." Bassanio has a large and influential circle of friends, and to contest this
declaration is to identify oneself as someone well outside that circle.
It thus "behoves" the reader to reclaim Bassanio's better nature. The
responsibility for good behavior lies not with the errant nobleman
but, rather, with the reader.

A second strategy used to ensure Bassanio's favorable reception
was rather less involved. With remarkable ease some commentators
on *The Merchant of Venice* simply reversed the order of events in the
play so that the betrothal of Portia and Bassanio takes place before
any talk of money occurs. Thus, Bassanio's poverty is taken to be
a sign of his goodness and misfortune, while the loan he seeks is
characterized not as that sought by a fortune hunter to facilitate his
wooing of a wealthy heiress but simply as that which is needed to
secure the happiness true hearts desire. "Bassanio is of noble birth
but poor," one editor claimed. "To carry out the arrangements for
his wedding he goes to his friend Antonio . . . and asks him for a
loan" (*Lines from the Poets* 7). Or, somewhat more elaborately, it was
recounted:

> A lovely Italian lady called Portia had many suitors, but
> the one whom she preferred was a young Venetian,
> named Bassanio. They were betrothed; but although she

was very rich, he was very poor. To carry out the
arrangements for his marriage, he asked money from a
young and prosperous merchant of Venice, called Antonio. (*Selections from Shakespeare* v)

It is perhaps not surprising, then, that there seems to be no mention anywhere of the obvious solution—namely, that the fabulously
wealthy Portia should pay for the wedding, which is, in fact, what
happens.

But there was an even more vexing question that commentators
on *The Merchant of Venice* had to face, and it was this. Despite having
so clearly set out the boundary between good and evil, and despite
having developed a system of signification so refined that within
its frame of reference even Bassanio could be made to seem like a
proper hero, most people then, as now, regularly mistook Shylock
for Antonio when they assumed, erroneously, that the title of the
play referred to him. The eponymous hero of *The Merchant of Venice*
is, of course, not Shylock but Antonio. But this fact seemed, repeatedly, to slip from people's minds. Naturally, the error was one that
commentators on the play took great pains to correct:

> The character of Antonio, the man of **Ancient Roman
> Honour,** and the Merchant Prince of Commercial
> Venice, is the pivot on which Venetian Society hinges,
> the centre round which it all turns. He it is who sup-
> ports the extravagance of the noble Bassanio, and whose
> stability is the foundation of the city's charter, and the
> city's freedom. . . . [T]hey altogether miss the spirit and
> meaning of the play who do not recognise that Antonio,
> *the royal merchant, the true gentleman,* the **dear lover** of
> Portia's **lord, the best conditioned and unwearied
> spirit in doing courtesies,** is the real hero of the play
> which is called by his name. (Barnett 12)

But, if Antonio were truly the man his impeccable credentials suggested he was, then how could anyone *possibly* get it wrong? How
could the real hero of *The Merchant of Venice,* the "pivot" of society,
the true gentleman, the man of "Ancient Roman Honour," possibly

be mistaken for anyone else, let alone a miserable, usurious Jew? The confusion here, I would argue, was clearly imported, for, while Shylock may have been the only Jew worth noticing in *The Merchant of Venice,* he was certainly not the only wealthy Jew to have commanded the attention of late Victorian society. Anxieties about wealthy Jews in the world outside the play were finding their way into the text.

I V

Up until the middle of the nineteenth century social relations in England were predominantly structured around the ownership of land, an arrangement that bore with it "power of a very special and all-pervading kind." Land ownership was highly profitable, the bias in taxation greatly favored landed over personal property, and the financial advantages associated with it "underpinned an unofficial hereditary control of church, army, government and everyday life" (Camplin 16). Landed status was also, effectively, a precondition of political power at Westminster, since both the House of Commons and the House of Lords were dominated by a "landed elite" well into the 1880s (18). Furthermore, a society structured in this way maintained powerful associations with an ideal of rural life closely connected to notions of tradition and rule by ancient and hereditary right. In short a society structured around the ownership of land promised tremendous stability in the long term.

But, as Jamie Camplin has argued, from the 1870s onward the balance of power began to shift. While the predominantly agricultural English economy had initially benefited from the technological changes wrought by the industrial revolution, profit from industry eventually overwhelmed profit derived from the land (29). Moreover, the rapid expansion of cities, the growth of professions such as law and banking, and the development of technologies such as the internal combustion engine, electric light, and those associated with the mass production of newspapers all contributed to a decline of the rural ideal and the importance of landed and hereditary privilege (32–36). As the city replaced the countryside as the seat of the elect and banking and finance came to replace landholding as the most important means of generating wealth, a new figure came to dominate late Victorian, but especially Edwardian, society. That figure was the plutocrat.

Distinct from both wealthy industrialists and from the swelling ranks of the middle classes, the plutocrats were perceived to be a breed apart. These were the men with a genius for making money, dedicated financiers who "had the will, and the resources, to drive for the top in an elitist struggle that dramatized the deep divisions in British society" and who amassed huge fortunes "at a speed which perhaps knew no precedent in the history of the world" (Camplin 38). In contrast with the traditional aristocracy, whose declining fortunes required that they modify their lifestyles, adopting a relatively inconspicuous manner, the plutocrats, suffering no such constraints, were legendary for their conspicuous, if not wildly excessive, displays of wealth.[14]

But the problem with the plutocrats, as the old guard saw it, was not simply one of vulgarity, although this was often and loudly decried. Rather, it was the extent to which their vulgar new money allowed them to assume both symbolic and real power. The purchase of ancient country houses from their indigent owners by wealthy newcomers, who required them only for the purpose of weekend entertaining, might be an affront to the English rural ideal. Similarly, the fact that the social circle of Edward VII was built around the plutocracy seemed to many a shocking, if not grotesque, development. But worst of all was the way in which such "social prestige, once achieved, was used as a means of entry to the institutions of government and influence," for "entry was the first step to dominance" (Camplin 111).

It was with the plutocratic entry into the institutional life of England that the real problem lay, not simply because these new "rulers" were not members of the traditional aristocracy but because so many of them were foreign in both the national and religious sense; in practice what the word *plutocrat* often meant was "wealthy foreign Jew." While it is a fact that "Jews were disproportionately well represented among the nation's very wealthy" (between 1870 and 1879, for example, "they accounted for 14 per cent of all British non-landed millionaires" [Feldman, *Englishmen and Jews* 78]), what is of essence here is the manner in which the contribution of wealthy Jews to the prosperity and governing of the nation was perceived to be a sinister development.[15] In the light of industrialization English society was changing, perhaps more rapidly and more drastically than many would have liked. The "chief protagonists" of this change were the plutocrats (Camplin 156), and the unease and suspicion with which these changes were met was frequently displaced onto them. "The Jews were said to have taken over society: an 'Israelitish army,' with its encampments in the City extending due west into Mayfair and thence north-west into Bedfordshire and Buckinghamshire." Indeed, by 1914 "England had experienced a Jewish Prime Minister, Lord Chancellor and Lord Chief Justice—and a Jacobson among the bishops of its national church" (Camplin 157).

Elite social status had once been inseparable from titles, bloodlines, inheritance, and the land. But titles could now be bought, fortunes could be made or lost in a single generation, and to the country squire the city seemed altogether overrun by an unvetted assembly of foreigners, interlopers, and arrivistes. Even more distressing was the fact that a disproportionate number of these interlopers—whether in the guise of members of Parliament or as the heads of financial dynasties—seemed to be Jews. Bargains could be struck between the aristocracy and the bourgeoisie so that gentlemen's clubs and public schools might be opened to meet the growing demands of the middle classes, but it was quite another matter for such bargains to be struck between the aristocracy and wealthy Jews. For, while the rule of plutocracy meant that Jews could now easily acquire the trappings of the elite, it failed to address the fact that, on the inside, Jews remained outsiders.[16] And in a society that increasingly valued wealth above traditional integrity it was only a matter of time before this fact would come home to roost.

A story by E. E. Bradford will serve to illustrate the point. "Manners Makyth Man: A Story of Winchester College" is one of a series of tales constituting the volume *Stories of Life at Our Great Public Schools,* each one deriving its title and its moral from a school's motto. This particular story focuses on the relationship between a stupid boy called Tubbs and his associate Meyer "whose curly black air [*sic*], oily skin, and hooked nose betrayed his Jewish origin" (23–24). While the two are generally unpopular, they are especially despised by another pair of boys called Anderson and Larker. Tubbs and Meyer, however, are the favorites of the master's loquacious wife, Alicia Cornwallis, who also happens to be Tubbs's aunt. Mrs. Cornwallis is a firm believer in the "gentle influence of refined feminine society" and to this end regularly invites boys to tea. The trouble begins when she invites both pairs of boys to tea at the same time.

At the table a joke is played on Anderson by his friend Larker, causing him to spill cream on the master's wife. All the boys are forced to stifle their laughter, but Meyer is heard quoting the school's motto, sotto voce, to ungentlemanly effect. "If 'Manners makyth Man,'" he says, "I am afraid that Anderson must be reckoned among the lower animals!" This remark subsequently leads Anderson to challenge Meyer to a fight, but the Jew, "in his most polished manner," denies ever having made it and refuses the challenge on the grounds that he disapproves of fighting (26). Anderson deals Meyer "a tremendous box on the ear" anyway, in the hope that witnessing this ignominy will, at least, persuade Tubbs to break off his association with the Jew. This last point is the crucial one because it is what the story is really about. The irritation is not simply that there is a Jew at the school or even that his manners are polished to the point of being unctuous but, rather, that someone, anyone, would deign to be his friend on whatever grounds. Bradford is meticulous in setting out Tubbs's reasons for associating with the Jew. Meyer, it so happens, is a hardened gambler, and, although Tubbs "was always abundantly supplied with cash, Meyer took care to get the larger share of it" (28). The Jew was "a regular spider" who had "got Tubbs into his web" and would "never leave him till he's sucked him dry!" (25).

Like another notorious Jewish speculator, Meyer one day initiates a gamble that may endanger his friend's life. Knowing that Tubbs cannot swim and that he is exceedingly clumsy to boot, Meyer bets him "an even fiver" that he can't walk across the river on some rotting and slippery boards. Tubbs accepts the challenge because,

> though Tubbs was a fool, he was far from being a coward. He had long been growing weary of his evil genius, and now all at once a vision of freedom gleamed before his eyes. If he won this fiver he could pay Meyer every farthing he owed him. "Done!" he cried recklessly, and without a moment's hesitation he set forth on his daring voyage. (29)

Against the odds Tubbs makes it safely across, but, heady with triumph, he foolishly attempts the return trip and falls into the river. Meyer's cowardice is immediately exposed, for, although he is "a first-rate swimmer, he was so paralysed with fear that he made no attempt to go in to the rescue, but stood on the bank shouting for help." Luckily, Anderson and Larker are in the vicinity and save the day. Tubbs goes home with his rescuer and "resolve[s] in his heart to pay Meyer in full on the first occasion, and never speak to him again" (30).

As one might naturally expect in such circumstances, Tubbs and Anderson now discuss their school motto. "I can't understand it," Tubbs says, "I think old Wykeham must be wrong in saying 'Manners makyth Man,' for . . . if you don't mind my saying so, Anderson, Meyer's manners are better than yours, but all the same they don't seem to have made a man of him!" Anderson is forced to explain that the manners in question are not "the sort of thing taught in young ladies' finishing schools or in books of etiquette, but something a little more solid, like the Latin *mores* or the French *moeurs*." Bradford is inclined to agree. "It is the way in which a fellow acts in real life, the manner in which he behaves under trial, that forms the character. And in this sense it is true that 'Manners Makyth Man'" (30–31).

Most obviously, the tale is a cautionary one signaling the dangers of admitting Jews into elite society. Although he is wealthy enough and, at least superficially, well mannered enough to attend Winchester College, Meyer can do little to hide his base inner nature. He preys on foolish boys, exploits the hospitality of naive hostesses, and takes the school's motto in vain. His gambling, like his ability to swindle the unsuspecting Tubbs, betrays a perverse manner of risk taking and an unnatural relationship to wealth. In fact, Meyer's interest in being at Winchester seems entirely based on the supply of victims it provides for his moneymaking schemes. The hypocrisy of his polished manner finds its typological fulfillment in his cowardice revealed in the moment of crisis. Where plutocracy rules, no one is safe, for in the absence of gentlemanly conduct there can be no effective self-regulation. Meyer may be numbered among the gentlemen of Winchester College, but he has a traitor's heart.

On second reading "Manners Makyth Man" appears remarkable for the ways in which it rehearses the great themes of *The Merchant of Venice*. The setting is a competitive and highly civilized society inhabited by men of varying abilities but governed by a common creed; whatever their shortcomings, these men are neither cowards nor cheats. Tubbs may be something of a fool, but it is with Antonio's love of risk taking and his laudable abandon that he sets forth on his "daring voyage" across the water in order to rid himself of his debt to the Jew. And who better than Meyer could fill the role of Shylock? True to form, he perverts the ideal of gentlemanly commerce to which the others so naturally subscribe. His love of money is the driving force of his existence and leads him blithely to gamble with the life of his friend. But, most important, Meyer makes a travesty of the school's motto. Like his Shakespearean prototype, he is prone to mistake the letter for the spirit of the law.

V

Summum jus summa injuria; the highest law, the highest injustice. Of all the morals derived from *The Merchant of Venice* this one seemed to be the key. For this was the moral that spoke the difference between the spirit and the letter of the law by pointing out that a common and too literal insistence on what is right could produce uncommon wrongs. Here at last, it seemed, was the stable boundary between Shylock and Antonio, between retribution and justice, and between citizens and the rest. Over and over again the moral was repeated like a litany for a troubled age. "What is the purpose of this play? . . . Summum jus, summa injuria, 'the highest law, the highest injustice'" (Barnett 11); "the idea underlying the whole play is contained in the Latin maxim, 'Summum jus summa injuria'" (Wood, Supplement 7); "the keynote to the . . . play is . . . contained in the old legal maxim *summum jus summa injuria*" (Wood, Manuals 33).

Although the outcome of *The Merchant of Venice* would have been well-known, there was something about the trial scene which seemed to set late Victorian readers of Shakespeare permanently on edge. Shylock's humiliation and defeat were certainties. But the mere fact that the Jew got as far as he did with his legal claim left readers decidedly ill at ease. It wasn't the memory of Antonio's brush with death that elicited this response but, rather, the fact that "Shylock checkmated and held at bay the whole state and legislature of Venice" (Crump 69). For, in taking his business to court, Shylock is seen not as pursuing a legitimate grievance or even as testing the claims of a putatively just society but, rather, as seeking to undermine the authority of the state by desecrating the rule of law. Shylock, one editor wrote, "standing on his rights, contained in the written law, the court is as it were out of very shame bound to entertain the question . . . how is the law to be evaded, or judicial murder prevented?" (Barnett 9). He "craftily places the redemption of his bond as necessary for the honour of the State of Venice," wrote another (Crook li).

Clearly, Shylock's deceptively simple demand that the law, *as written*, be obeyed, triggered a crisis at the very heart of late Victorian liberalism. For, in claiming his pound of flesh, he tests not just the meaning of the letter of the law but also the typological practice of reading which underpins the whole edifice of liberal justice. Some people can read sacred texts and understand them; other people cannot. Thus, it was argued that, while

> Shylock reasons well and logically according to the principles of the Mosaic religion in which he has been brought up he only knows the letter of the law, and [so] understands no doctrine higher than that of an eye for an eye and a tooth for a tooth. (Wood, *Manuals* 24)

Moreover, Shylock's call for justice according to the letter of the law reduces liberal justice to its own brand of sophistry when, forced to concede the pound of flesh, it saves Antonio and its own honor only by adding the proviso that Shylock may have his pound of flesh but no drop of blood. The "legal quibble" by which the Jew is eventually defeated thus secures the necessary outcome but does little to erase the memory of how close to the brink Venetian justice had come. It was commonly remarked that a lesser writer than Shakespeare might not have salvaged the situation and that only "the hand of genius," a deus ex machina, had "loosened the Gordian knot" and saved the day (Barnett 9). Hence, the obsessive return to the Latin maxim in an attempt to keep the edifice intact. *Summum jus, summa injuria.*

Some people would understand the distinction between the letter and the spirit of the law; others, like Shylock, would not.

"There is an old saying," wrote John Earle, "that justice over-strained becomes injustice. The ancients embodied it in a well-known proverb: *Summum jus summa injuria.*"

> Now this is not, and cannot be, true of the great and pure Justice where it issues free and spiritual from its divine fountain; it is only true of justice as represented in this nether world, where it is embodied in rigid forms, such as these which we call Law, conventional propriety, and social maxims . . . Useful as these are for practical application . . . when extraordinary cases arise, they are found inapplicable, or if forcibly applied . . . occasion a wretched mockery of justice.

In other words the challenge that *The Merchant of Venice* sets for us, Earle argued, is the one of knowing when to bend the rules and follow the spirit rather than the letter of the law. "The law is *for* Shylock," he admits, yet

> the reader, who is a friend of law and order . . . finds himself . . . siding with Bassanio, when he would have the judge just *wrest the law a little* . . . In short, we feel that in these instances, Truth has changed her seat, and is no longer posted at the side of Law. (xii)

Shylock could live in Venice, ply his trade, strike his bargains, and demand that they be honored. He could even have his day in court, but he could never win. For, although "Shylock has the letter of the law upon his side, [as] Portia endeavours to point out to him . . . true morality," in a liberal society, rests "not upon right and law, as the Jew supposed, but upon divine grace" (Wood, Manuals 33). Or, as Stanley Wood so plainly demonstrated, playing the winning card for generations of educators, "a proper social system must be based not upon human laws and right alone, but upon right and law interpreted by Christian conciliatory love, and tempered by a mediating mercy" (Supplement 7). The Christian society in which a Jew could not be a fellow countryman and the liberal state in which the law held true for friend and alien alike were not, then, so different after all.

Shylock had had his day in court, but "the law he had craved for now held him, not his victim, fast, and that wise young judge, who had prayed him to show mercy, now showed him justice. He had conspired against the life of a citizen—he, an alien, and there again the law held him" (Maud and Maud 296).

It was a story you could tell your children, a tale as enduring as the myth of creation itself. Like all good stories, it had its moments of unease and its moments of trepidation, but, ultimately, it was a story that could be safely told. For, as everyone knew, in the end "Shylock was beaten at last, his money all taken from him, his wicked, cruel plan defeated; and he crawled out of the Court like the cowardly sneak that he was" (Gordon 95).

Notes

INTRODUCTION

1.   Although it will not be possible here to enter into a full-length discussion of which Shakespeare plays were deemed most suitable for children at the time, the question of exclusion throws the popularity of *The Merchant* even further into relief, since it was widely considered to be free of the difficulties that compromised the educational suitability of so many of the other plays. For contemporary opinion on the question, see English Association, *The Teaching of Shakespeare in Secondary Schools*, Pamphlet no. 2 (n.d.) (British Library Catalogue AC 2664); Board of Education, *Suggestions for the Teaching of English* (London: HMSO, 1912); John Dover Wilson, *Humanism in the Continuation School*, Board of Education Pamphlet no. 43 (London: HMSO, 1921); *The Teaching of English in England*, Newbolt Report (London: HMSO, 1921).

2.   For an overview of these commissions of inquiry and subsequent reforms, see Stuart J. Maclure, *Educational Documents: England and Wales, 1816–1963* (London: Chapman and Hall, 1965); and John Lawson and Harold Silver, *A Social History of Education in England* (London: Methuen, 1973). For the period just prior to the 1870 Education Act, see Norman Morris, "State Paternalism and *Laissez-faire* in the 1860s," *Studies in the Government and Control of Education since 1860* (London: Methuen, 1970). See also Harold Silver, "Education, Opinion and the 1870s," *Education as History* (London: Methuen, 1983); and Michael Sanderson, *Education, Economic Change and Society in England, 1780–1870* (London: Macmillan, 1983). On the 1870 Education Act, see Eric Rich, *The Education Act 1870: A Study of Public Opinion* (London: Longman, 1970). On working-class education prior to the 1870s, see Richard Johnson, "Educational Policy and Social Control in Early Victorian England,"

Past and Present 49 (1970): 96–119; "Notes on the Schooling of the English Working Class, 1780–1850," in *Schooling and Capitalism,* ed. Roger Dale, Geoff Esland, and Madeleine MacDonald (London: Routledge, 1976), 44–54; and "'Really Useful Knowledge': Radical Education and Working-Class Culture, 1790–1848," in *Working-Class Culture,* ed. John Clarke, Chas Critcher, and Richard Johnson (London: Hutchinson, 1979), 75–102.

3.   For the history of English literature as an academic discipline, see Chris Baldick, *The Social Mission of English Criticism, 1848–1932* (Oxford: Clarendon P, 1987); Terry Eagleton, "The Rise of English" in *Literary Theory* (Oxford: Blackwell, 1983); Brian Doyle, *English and Englishness* (London; Routledge, 1989). Also of interest are Brian Doyle, "Against the Tyranny of the Past," *Red Letters* 10 (n.d.): 23–33; and "The Hidden History of English Studies," in *Re-reading English,* ed. Peter Widdowson (London: Methuen, 1982): 17–31; Tony Davies, "Education, Ideology and Literature," *Red Letters* 7 (n.d.); 4–15; Noel King, "'The Teacher Must Exist before the Pupil': The Newbolt Report on the Teaching of English in England, 1921," *Literature and History* 13.1 (1987): 14–37; and Robert Holton, "'A True Bond of Unity': Popular Education and the Foundation of the Discipline of English Literature in England," *Dalhousie Review* 66.1–2 (1986): 31–44. For an earlier account of the study of English, see D. J. Palmer, *The Rise of English Studies* (London: Oxford UP, 1965). On the study of English literature in a colonial context, see Gauri Viswanathan, "The Beginnings of English Literary Study in British India," *Oxford Literary Review* 9 (1987): 2–26; and Ania Loomba, *Gender, Race, Renaissance Drama* (Manchester: Manchester UP, 1989), esp. intro. and chap. 1. A classic statement on English literature and the education of women remains Charles Kingsley's "On English Literature," originally delivered as an inaugural address at Queen's College, London, in 1848. Although it therefore predates the period with which this book is mainly concerned, the lecture had tremendous currency in the latter decades of the century and was often quoted and reprinted, as in his collected *Literary and General Essays* (London: Macmillan, 1890), 245–65.

4.   See, for example, Joan N. Burstyn, *Victorian Education and the Ideal of Womanhood* (New Brunswick, NJ: Rutgers UP, 1984); Anna Davin, "'Mind That You Do as You Are Told': Reading Books for Board School Girls, 1870–1902," *Feminist Review* 3 (1979): 89–98; and "Imperialism and Motherhood," *History Workshop Journal* 5 (1978): 9–66; Sarah Delamont and Lorna Duffin, *The Nineteenth-Century Woman* (London: Croom Helm,

1978); Carol Dyhouse, *Girls Growing Up in Late Victorian and Edwardian England* (London: RKP, 1981); "Social Darwinistic Ideas and the Development of Women's Education in England, 1880–1920, *History of Education* 5 (1976): 41–58; and "Towards a 'Feminine' Curriculum for English Schoolgirls: The Demands of Ideology, 1870–1963," *Women's Studies International Quarterly* 1 (1978): 297–311; Felicity Hunt, ed., *Lessons for Life: The Schooling of Girls and Women, 1850–1950* (Oxford: Blackwell, 1987); Deborah Gorham, *The Victorian Girl and the Feminine Ideal* (London: Croom Helm, 1982); June Purvis, "Social Class, Education and Ideals of Femininity in the Nineteenth Century," in *Gender and the Politics of Schooling,* ed. Madeleine Arnot and Gaby Weiner (London: Open UP, 1987), 254–75; Carolyn Steedman, "'The Mother Made Conscious': The Historical Development of a Primary School Pedagogy," *History Workshop Journal* 20 (1985): 149–63; Ann Marie Wolpe, "The Official Ideology of Education for Girls," in *Educability, Schools and Ideology,* ed. Michael Flude and John Ahier (London: Croom Helm, 1974), 138–59.

5.   For the New Women, see Lucy Bland, *Banishing the Beast: English Femininity and Sexual Morality, 1885–1914* (London: Penguin, 1995). See also Juliet Gardner, *The New Woman* (London: Collins and Brown, 1993).

6.   For the changing face of nineteenth-century Anglo-Jewry, see David Feldman, *Englishmen and Jews* (London: Yale UP, 1994); and Bill Williams, "The Anti-Semitism of Tolerance: Middle-Class Manchester and the Jews, 1870–1900," in *City, Class and Culture: Studies of Social Policy and Cultural Production in Victorian Manchester,* ed. Alan J. Kidd and K. W. Roberts (Manchester: Manchester UP, 1985), 74–102. On immigration, see Feldman, *Englishmen and Jews,* chaps. 6–7; Lloyd P. Gartner, *The Jewish Immigrant in England, 1870–1914* (London: Simon, 1960); and John Garrard, *The English and Immigration, 1880–1910* (London: Oxford UP, 1971).

7.   For wealthy Jews, see W. D. Rubenstein, "Jews among Top British Wealth Holders, 1857–1969: Decline of the Golden Age," *Jewish Social Studies* 34 (1972): 73–84. For the Jewish Plutocracy, see Jamie Camplin, *The Rise of the Plutocrats* (London: Constable, 1978).

8.   On the images of the alien and the plutocrat, see Kenneth Lunn, "Political Anti-Semitism before 1914: Fascism's Heritage?" in *British Fascism: Essays on the Radical Right in Inter-War Britain,*

ed. Kenneth Lunn and Richard C. Thurlow (London: Croom Helm, 1980), 20–40.

CHAPTER 1

1.   The word first appears in the preface to *Plays for Puritans* (1900).

2.   For bardolatry, see Howard Felperin, "Bardolatry Then and Now," in *The Appropriation of Shakespeare: Post Renaissance Reconstructions of the Works and the Myth,* ed. Jean Marsden (Hemel Hempstead: Harvester, 1991), 129–44; and "Historicizing Bardolatry: Or, Where Could Coleridge Have Been Coming From?" *The Uses of the Canon: Elizabethan Literature and Contemporary Theory* (Oxford: Clarendon P, 1990), 1–15. See also Terence Hawkes, *That Shakespearian Rag* (London: Methuen, 1986); and Graham Holderness, ed., *The Shakespeare Myth* (Manchester: Manchester UP, 1988). Still extremely useful among older writings are R. W. Babcock's *The Genesis of Shakespeare Idolatry, 1766–1799* (Chapel Hill: U of North Carolina P, 1931); and F. E. Halliday's, *The Cult of Shakespeare* (London: Duckworth, 1951). Of recent works on the institutionalization of Shakespeare, see especially Jonathan Bate, *Shakespearean Constitutions: Politics, Theatre, Criticism, 1730–1830* (Oxford: Clarendon P, 1989); Margreta De Grazia, *Shakespeare Verbatim: The Reproduction of Authenticity and the 1790 Apparatus* (Oxford: Oxford UP, 1991); and Michael Dobson, *The Making of the National Poet: Shakespeare, Adaptation and Authorship, 1660–1769* (Oxford: Clarendon P, 1992).

3.   See, for example, Jonathan Bate, *Shakespearean Constitutions* (Oxford: Clarendon P, 1989); Christine Deelman, *The Great Shakespeare Jubilee* (London: Michael Joseph, 1964); Michael Dobson, *The Making of the National Poet* (Oxford, Calrendon P, 1992).

4.   A detailed study of the role of the clergy in Shakespeare celebrations falls outside the scope of this study. A preliminary indication of the scale of clerical importance to the endeavor, however, may be gained from the lists of participants in the preparations given in the *Athenæum* in 1863–64.

5.   My view of Coleridge and Shakespeare is substantially informed by the ideas of John Barrell.

CHAPTER 2

1.   See for example: Anna Davin, "Imperialism and Motherhood," *History Workshop Journal* 5 (1978): 9–66; Jane Mackay and

Pat Thane, "The Englishwoman," in *Englishness: Politics and Culture 1880–1920*, ed. Robert Colls and Philip Dodd. (London: Croom Helm, 1986), 191–229; Jane Lewis, *The Politics of Motherhood: Child and Maternal Welfare in England, 1900–1939* (London: Croom Helm, 1980); Lorna Duffin, "Prisoners of Progress: Women and Evolution," in *The Nineteenth-Century Woman*, ed. Sarah Delamont and Lorna Duffin (London: Croom Helm, 1978), 57–91; Carol Dyhouse, "Social Darwinistic Ideas and the Development of Women's Education in England, 1880–1920," *History of Education* 5.1 (1976): 41–58.

2.   Anna Jameson's book, though first published in 1832, went through numerous reprints, including several editions in the 1890s and early 1900s.

CHAPTER 3

1.   On spectacular production, see Michael Booth, *Victorian Spectacular Theatre, 1850–1910* (London: RKP, 1981); Richard Foulkes, ed., *Shakespeare and the Victorian Stage* (Cambridge: Cambridge UP, 1986), esp. "Part 1: Shakespeare in the Picture Frame"; William E. Kleb. "Shakespeare in Tottenham-Street: An 'Aesthetic' *Merchant of Venice*," *Theatre Survey* 16.2 (1975): 97–121.

2.   The dominance of Irving's interpretation is further indicated by the fact that no notable production of the *Merchant* which did not feature Irving in the role of Shylock was mounted in London until 1905. For a complete list of notable productions and revivals, see Freda Gaye, ed., *Who's Who in the Theatre* (London: Pitman, 1967), 1434. For a more general overview of Jews on the late Victorian stage, see Shearer West, "The Construction of Racial Type: Caricature, Ethnography, and Jewish Physiognomy in Fin-de-Siècle Melodrama," *Nineteenth Century Theatre* 21.1 (1993): 4–40.

3.   Irving's first public defense of his Shylock appeared in *Theatre* on 1 Dec. 1879 (254–55), as part of a symposium on the character. For a lengthy reassertion of his original intentions several years into the history of the production, see Joseph Hatton, *Henry Irving's Impressions of America*, vol. 1 (London: Sampson Low, Marston, Searle and Rivington, 1884), 262–75.

4.   John Gross's claim that "it is generally agreed that his [Irving's] interpretation grew less sympathetic over the years" (141) is unsupported by any convincing evidence. Virtually the only critic to express this view was William Winter, a notorious American theater critic and by Gross's own admission an extremist, who

was known as an arch-conservative and a bigot, consistently antagonistic toward non-Anglo-Saxon foreigners on the American stage (*Oxford Companion to the Theatre* 897). Winter's account of Irving's Shylock, in *Shakespeare on the Stage,* appears to be Gross's source. But what Gross fails to take into account is Winter's own reading of *The Merchant* by which he then measures the legitimacy or illegitimacy of subsequent interpretations of Shylock's role. The lurid language Winter uses to describe his ideal of a convincing Jew, coupled with his belief that "the true Shylock of Shakespeare" must be "hard, merciless, inexorable, terrible" (178), strongly suggests that Irving's softening of the role did not sit well with Winter's own feelings about Jews. The two men were friends for many years, and it is likely that Winter was reading into Irving's performance what he wished were there but, as other evidence would suggest, manifestly was not.

5.   For a selection of reviews of Irving's American tour of 1883, see *Mr. Henry Irving and Miss Ellen Terry in America: Opinions of the Press* (Chicago: John Morris, 1884).

6.   Edward Moore, in his essay "Henry Irving's Shakespearean Productions" (*Theatre Survey* 17.2 [1976]: 201), says, for example, that Irving "cared nothing about realizing a play as written, but only about making his effects; and splendid as these no doubt were, most of us would rather have Shakespeare's."

7.   On the importance of conversion as a cultural motif and of the father-daughter relationship in this context, see Michael Ragussis's compelling *Figures of Conversion: "The Jewish Question" and English National Identity* (Durham: Duke UP, 1995).

8.   Robert Hichens, in his essay "Irving as Shylock" (in *We Saw Him Act,* ed. H. A. Saintsbury and Cecil Palmer [London: Hurst and Blackett, 1939], 168), remarks on how unforgettable this bit of stage business was.

9.   For an example of just such a discussion, see Frederick Hawkins, "The Character of Shylock," *Theatre* (1 Nov. 1879): 191–98; and the roundtable discussion involving numerous commentators, including Irving himself, the following month (*Theatre* [1 Dec. 1879]).

10.   For a recent account of Lopez, see David Katz, "The Jewish Conspirators of Elizabethan England" *The Jews in the History of England, 1485–1850* (Oxford: Clarendon P, 1994): 49–106.

11. See also, Sander Gilman. *Jewish Self-Hatred* (Baltimore: Johns Hopkins UP, 1986): 37 ff., 61 ff.

12. On changing perceptions of Marranism, see Miriam Bodian, "'Men of the Nation': The Shaping of *Converso* Identity in Early Modern Europe," *Past and Present* 143 (1994): 48–76.

13. See Gilman, *Jewish Self-Hatred,* chap. 3, esp. 83 ff.

14. On this point, see also Moshe Lazar, "'Scorched Parchments and Tortured Memories': The 'Jewishness' of the Anussim (Crypto-Jews)," in *Cultural Encounters: The Impact of the Inquisition in Spain and the New World,* ed. Mary Elizabeth Perry and Anne J. Cruz (Berkeley: U of California P, 1991), 182 ff.

15. See Arthur Dimock, "The Conspiracy of Dr. Lopez," *English Historical Review* (July 1894): 440–72; and John W. Hales, "Shakespeare and the Jews," *English Historical Review* (Oct. 1894): 652–61.

16. See C. H. Firth, *Sir Sidney Lee, 1859–1926,* in Proceedings of the British Academy (London: Humphrey Milford, 1929), 15:3.

17. *Bassanio:*
Let me choose,

For as I am, I live upon the rack.
Portia:
Upon the rack Bassanio? Then confess
What treason there is mingled with your love.
Bassanio:
None but that ugly treason of mistrust
Which makes me fear th'enjoying of my love.
There may as well be amity and life
'Tween snow and fire, as treason and my love.
Portia:
Ay, but I fear you speak upon the rack,
Where men enforced do speak anything.
Bassanio:
Promise me life and I'll confess the truth.
Portia:
Well then, confess and live.

(III.ii.25–39)

CHAPTER 4

1. Adult versions of educational texts were similarly geared for home study and self-improvement or for use by amateur dramatic societies.

2.   The standard authority on this subject remains F. J. Harvey Darton, *Children's Books in England* (1932; reprint, Cambridge: Cambridge UP, 1982); but see also Kimberley Reynolds, *Girls Only? Gender and Popular Fiction in Britain, 1880–1910* (London: Harvester, 1990).

3.   For an overview of these changes, see Brian Alderson, "Tracts, Rewards and Fairies: The Victorian Contribution to Children's Literature," in *Essays in the History of Publishing, in Celebration of the 250th Anniversary of the House of Longman,* ed. Asa Briggs (London: Longman, 1974), 245–82.

4.   Numbers are comparable for several other individual plays, in addition to scores of selected and collected editions. The catalog of the Birmingham Shakespeare Library may be consulted for a sense of the scale of production involved.

5.   This observation is supported by the *Oxford Companion to Children's Literature* (ed. Humphrey Carpenter and Mari Prichard [Oxford: Oxford UP, 1984], 481), and a substantial list of childrens' versions of Shakespeare issued during this period is included in the first section of my bibliography. Charles and Mary Lamb's *Tales* were also continually republished at this time, with nearly sixty British editions of the *Tales* appearing between 1873 and 1920.

6.   The text that Earle cites as an example is Bacon's essay "On Usury."

7.   For examples of Christian and Christian socialist arguments against usury, see William Blissard, *The Ethic of Usury and Interest* (London: Swan Sonnenschein, 1892); Edward Carpenter, *Modern Money-Lending* (London: John Heywood, 1883); R. F. Crawford, *Letters and Leaflets on Usury . . .* (London: R. F. Crawford, 1889); W. Cunningham, *Christian Opinion on Usury* (Edinburgh: Macmillan, 1884); E. W. Mason, *The Forgotten Teaching and Neglected Discipline of the Church as to Usury* (Leicester: Co-operative Printing Society, 1900); R. G. Sillar, *Usury: A Paper Read before Some Members of the University of Cambridge . . .* (London: Exeter Hall, 1885).

8.   The committee was chaired by Serjeant Onslow and met from 30 April to 22 May 1818.

9.   For a summary of these changes, see Hugh Bellot and James Willis, *The Law Relating to Unconscionable Bargains with Money-Lenders* (London: Stevens and Haynes, 1897), 29–31; and

F. W. Read, *Evils of State Interference with Money Lending* (London: Watts and Co., 1896), 5.

10. The committee of 1897 was chaired by T. W. Russell and met from 13 May to 29 July 1897.

11. The legal implications of this important distinction are discussed at length by Justice John Byles, *Observations on the Usury Laws . . .* (London: S. Sweet, 1845). See also Bellot and Willis, *Law,* ix.

12. Farrow served as honorary secretary to the Agricultural Banks Association, a "philanthropic body . . . established to encourage the formation of village credit societies in England" (*British Parliamentary Papers: Report from the Select Committee on Money Lending,* vol. 10 [London: HMSO, 1897], 415), in effect an association devoted to keeping farmers out of the debt of unscrupulous landlords.

13. The importance of this shift in terms of the history of legal attempts to regulate moneylending is discussed by Haythorne Reed, in *A Commentary on the Law Relating to Money-Lenders and the Money-Lenders Act, 1900* (London: Waterlow Bros., 1900).

14. See Jamie Camplin, *The Rise of the Plutocrats* (London: Constable, 1978), esp. chaps. 6–7.

15. In addition to David Feldman, *Englishmen and Jews* (New Haven: Yale UP, 1994), 78–82, see W. D. Rubinstein, "Jews among Top British Wealth Holders, 1857–1969," *Jewish Social Studies* 34 (1972): 73–84; and *Men of Property: The Very Wealthy in Britain since the Industrial Revolution* (London: Croom Helm, 1981). On the fall of the traditional aristocracy, see David Cannadine, *The Decline and Fall of the British Aristocracy* (New Haven: Yale UP, 1990); and J. V. Beckett, *The Aristocracy in England, 1660–1914* (Oxford: Blackwell, 1986). Also of interest are Richard Davis, *The English Rothschilds* (Chapel Hill: U of North Carolina P, 1983); Anne and Roger Cowen, *Victorian Jews through British Eyes* (Oxford: Oxford UP, 1986); and A. Rubens, "The Rothschilds in Caricature," *Transactions of the Jewish Historical Society of England* 20 (1968–69): 76–87.

16. This dynamic is well illustrated by Stephen Doree, in his article "The Sassoons of Trent Park," *Heritage,* ed. Jewish Research Group of the Edmonton Historical Society, vol. 1 (London: Edmonton Historical Society, 1982), n.p.

Bibliography

PRIMARY SOURCES
Examination and Study Guides and Other Editions of Shakespeare and The Merchant of Venice

Barnett, T. Duff, ed. *Shakespeare's Merchant of Venice.* London: Bell, 1893.

Baughan, Rosa, ed. *Shakespeare's Plays. Abridged and Revised for the Use of Girls.* London: Allman, 1863.

———. *Shakespeare's Plays. Abridged and Revised for the Use of Girls.* 2d ed. London: Washbourne, 1871.

The Comedy of The Merchant of Venice. Blackie's School Classics. London: Blackie, 1879.

Crook, C. W., ed. *The Merchant of Venice.* London: Ralph, Holland, 1907.

Crump, Geoffrey. *A Guide to the Study of Shakespeare's Plays.* London: Harrap, 1925.

Earle, John, ed. *The Most Excellent Historie of* The Merchant of Venice . . . *Abbreviated and Adapted for Social Reading in Parts by the Swanswick Shakespeare Circle.* London: Longman, 1862.

Gordon, Adelaide C. "The Merchant of Venice." *Phoebe's Shakespeare Arranged for Children.* London: Bickers, 1894.

Hoffman, Alice. *Stories from Shakespeare's Plays for Children.* London: Dent, 1904.

———. *The Children's Shakespeare.* London: Dent, 1911.

Hudson, Robert. *Tales from Shakespeare.* London: Collins, 1907.

Hunter, Rev. J. *Examination Questions on the First Two Books of Milton's Paradise Lost, and on Shakespeare's Merchant of Venice.* London: Longman, 1862.

Lang, Jean. *Stories from Shakspeare Told to the Children.* London: Jack, 1905.

Lang, Leonora. *Gateway to Shakespeare.* London: Nelson, 1908.

Lines from the Poets: With Notes for Use in Elementary and Secondary Schools. No. 6: *Shakespeare's* Merchant of Venice. London: National Society's Depository, 1879.

Macleod, Mary. *The Shakespeare Story-Book.* London: Wells, Gardner, 1902.

Mais, S. P. B. *An English Course for Everybody*. London: Richards, 1921.

Maltby, S. E., ed. *The Merchant of Venice*. Kings Treasuries Edition. Gen. ed. Sir A. T. Quiller-Couch. London: Dent, 1921.

Marshall, F. A., and Henry Irving, eds. *The Merchant of Venice. The Henry Irving Shakespeare*. London: Blackie, 1888.

Maud, Constance, and Mary Maud. *The Merchant of Venice. Shakespeare's Stories*. London: Arnold, 1913.

Meiklejohn, J. M. D., ed. *Shakespeare's* Merchant of Venice. London: Chambers, 1879.

Merchant, W. Moelwyn, ed. *The Merchant of Venice*. London: Penguin, 1967.

The Merchant of Venice. As presented at the Lyceum Theatre under the Management of Mr. Henry Irving. London: Chiswick, 1881.

Nesbit, Edith. *The Children's Shakespeare*. London: Tuck, 1897.

Parry, Thomas, ed. *Shakespeare's* Merchant of Venice. London: Longman, 1883.

Quiller-Couch, Arthur. *Historical Tales from Shakespeare*. London: Arnold, 1899.

Seamer, Mary. *Shakespeare's Stories Simply Told*. London: Thomas Nelson, 1880.

Shakespeare, William. *The Children's Shakespeare*. London: Macmillan, 1910.

Shakespeare's Merchant of Venice *for Schools and Students Preparing for Examination*. Gill's Oxford and Cambridge Series. London: Gill, 1886.

Stidolph, Ada Baynes. *The Children's Shakespeare*. London: Allman, 1902.

The Trial from Shakespeare's Merchant of Venice. London: Moffatt, 1875.

"The Trial of Antonio." *Selections from Shakespeare*. Allman's English Classics for Elementary Schools. London: Allman, 1874.

Verity, A. W., ed. *The Merchant of Venice*. Cambridge: Cambridge University Press, 1912.

Wood, Stanley. Supplement to *The Merchant of Venice. Questions and Notes*. Dinglewood Shakespeare Manuals. Manchester: Heywood, 1891.

———. *The Merchant of Venice. Questions and Notes*. Dinglewood Shakespeare Manuals. Manchester: Heywood, 1897.

Woods, Mary A. "The Story of the Caskets and Rings from *The Merchant of Venice*." *Scenes from Shakespeare for Use in Schools*. London: Macmillan, 1898.

Wykes, C. H. *The Shakespeare Reader; Being Extracts from the Plays of Shakespeare Specially Selected as Fulfilling Article 28 and Schedule IV of the Education Code*. London: Blackie, 1880.

Unsigned Articles

"The Alien Immigrant." *Blackwood's Magazine* Jan. 1903: 132–41.

"At the Play." *Theatre* 1 Dec. 1879: 292–98.

"Essay Writing on a Great English Author—My Favourite Heroine from Shakespeare." *Girl's Own Paper* 10 Mar. 1888: 380–81.

"Foreign Undesirables." *Blackwood's Magazine* Feb. 1901: 279–89.

"The Girl's Own Order of Merit." *Girl's Own Paper* 8 Oct. 1887: 8.

"The Jewish Workman." *Social Democrat* Jan. 1898: 19–20.

"The Modern Jew." *Quarterly Review* Jan. 1896: 29–57.

"Our Omnibus-Box." *Theatre* 1 Jan. 1880: 62–64.

"Our Omnibus-Box." *Theatre* 1 Mar. 1880: 188.

"Our Prize Competitions: Essay Writing on a Great English Author." *Girl's Own Paper* 8 Oct. 1887: 32.

"Our Representative Man." *Punch* 15 Nov. 1879: 225–26.

"The Portion of Portia." *Punch* 2 May 1900: 320.

"Problems of Anglicisation." *Jewish Annual* (1943–44): 73–82.

"Religion in Literature." *Edinburgh Review* Jan. 1908: 178–202.

Review. 21 May 1887. Publication unknown. Production file for Irving's *Merchant of Venice*. Enthoven Collection. Theatre Museum. Covent Garden, London.

"Shylock at the Lyceum." *Truth* 6 Nov. 1879: 568–69.

"Theatrical Reform: The 'Merchant of Venice' at the Lyceum." *Blackwood's Edinburgh Magazine* Dec. 1879: 641–56.

"Was Shakespeare a Roman Catholic?" *Edinburgh Review* Jan. 1866: 146–85.

"The Week." *Athenæum* 8 Nov. 1879: 605.

Parliamentary Papers

British Parliamentary Papers: Report from the Select Committee on Money Lending. Vol. 10. London: HMSO, 1897.

British Parliamentary Papers: Report from the Select Committee on Money Lending. Vol. 11. London: HMSO, 1898.

British Parliamentary Papers: Report from the Select Committee on the Usury Laws. Vol. 6. London: HMSO, 1818.

British Parliamentary Papers on Education. Vols. 17, 22. Shannon: Irish UP, 1969.

Other Primary Sources

Adler, Hermann. "Can Jews Be Patriots?" *Nineteenth Century* Apr. 1878: 637–46.

———. "Jews and Judaism: A Rejoinder." *Nineteenth Century* July 1878: 133–50.

Anderson, David. "The Character of Shylock." *Theatre* 1 Dec. 1879: 259–60.

Anderson, Robert. "The Problem of the Criminal Alien." *Nineteenth Century* Feb. 1911: 217–24.

Anon. *Religious and Moral Sentences from Shakespeare Compared with Sacred Passages Drawn from Holy Writ.* London: Calkin and Budd, 1843.

Arbuthnot, George, ed. *Shakespeare Sermons*. London: Longmans, Green, 1900.

Aronides. "The Problem before Anglo-Jewry." *Contemporary Review* July 1912: 57–65.

B. A. "Shakespeare's Use of the Bible." *Cassell's Family Magazine* (1879): 490–92.

Bacon, Sir Francis. "Of Usury." *Bacon's Essays*. London: Longman, 1899. 442–48.

Barry, William. "The Catholic Strain in Shakespeare." I. Gollancz, *Book* 31–34.

Beeching, H. C. "The Shakespeare Sermon." Reprinted in Stratford-upon-Avon *Herald* 28 Apr. 1911.

———. "The Teaching of English Literature." *Essays on Secondary Education*. Ed. Christopher Cookson. Oxford: Clarendon, 1898. 214–31.

Bell, James. *Biblical and Shakespearian Characters Compared*. London: Simpkin, Marshall, Hamilton, Kent, 1894.

Bellamy, G. Somers. *Shaksperian Sermons*, nos. 1–10 (magazine articles). Birmingham Shakespeare Library Collection 1877.

Bellot, Hugh, and James Willis. *The Law Relating to Unconscionable Bargains with Money-Lenders*. London: Stevens and Haynes, 1897.

Benjamin, Lewis S. "The Passing of the English Jew." *Nineteenth Century* Sept. 1912: 491–504.

Bentham, Jeremy. "Defence of Usury." *The Works of Jeremy Bentham*. Vol. 3. Edinburgh: Tait, 1843.

Birch, W. J. *An Inquiry into the Philosophy and Religion of Shakspere*. London: C. Mitchell, 1848.

Blissard, William. *The Ethic of Usury and Interest*. London: Swan Sonnenschein, 1892.

Board of Education. *Differentiation of Curriculum for Boys and Girls Respectively in Secondary Schools*. London: HMSO, 1923.

———. *Suggestions for the Teaching of English*. London: HMSO, 1912.

———. "The Teaching of English in Secondary Schools." Circular no. 753. London: HMSO, 1910.

Bowden, Henry Sebastien. *The Religion of Shakespeare*. London: Burns and Oates, 1899.

Bradford, E. E. "Manners Makyth Man." *Stories of Life at Our Great Public Schools*. London: Stockwell, 1908. 23–31.

Bradley, Henry. "Shakespeare and the English Language." I. Gollancz, *Book* 106–9.

Brown, James. *Bible Truths with Shaksperian Parallels*. London: Whittaker, 1862.

Browne, G. F. "The Use of Works of Fiction" (23 Apr. 1893). Arbuthnot 1–21.

Bruce, Lenny. *The Essential Lenny Bruce.* New York: Ballantine, 1967.

Buckland, Anna. *The Teaching of English Literature.* London: n.p., 1885.

Bullock, Charles. *Shakspeare's Debt to the Bible.* London: Hand and Heart, 1879.

Burgess, William. *The Bible in Shakespeare.* Chicago: Winona, 1903.

Byles, John. *Observations on the Usury Laws . . . .* London: Sweet, 1845.

Carlyle, A. J. *The Shakspeare Tercentenary: A Sermon Preached in the City Church of Oxford, 30 April, 1916.* Oxford: Blackwell, 1916.

Carpenter, Edward. *Modern Money-Lending.* London: Heywood, 1883.

Carpenter, W. B. *Shakespeare: A Gift from God.* Tercentenary Sermon preached in Westminster Abbey. Reprinted in *Guardian* 4 May 1916: 382–83.

Carter, Thomas. *Shakespeare and Holy Scripture.* London: Hodder and Stoughton, 1905.

Cecil, Arthur. "The Trial Scene." *Theatre* 1 Jan. 1880: 53–55.

Chesterton, G. K. "Shakespeare and the Legal Lady." *Fancies versus Fads.* London: Methuen, 1923.

Clarke, Mary Cowden. *Complete Concordance to Shakespeare.* London: Knight, 1845.

——. *The Girlhood of Shakespeare's Heroines.* 2 vols. London: Dent, 1850–52.

——. "Shakespeare as the Girl's Friend." *Girl's Own Paper* 4 June 1887: 562–64.

Coleridge, Samuel Taylor. *Biographia Literaria.* 2 vols. Ed. J. Shawcross. London: Oxford UP, 1958.

——. *Coleridge on Shakespeare: The Text of the Lectures of 1811–12.* Ed. R. A. Foakes. London: RKP, 1971.

——. "Essay IV." "Essays on the Principles of Method." *Collected Works of Samuel Taylor Coleridge.* Ed. Barbara E. Rooke. London: RKP, 1969. 4:448–57.

——. *Shakespearean Criticism.* 2 vols. Ed. Thomas Middleton Raysor. London: Dent, 1960.

Collins, John Churton. "The Religion of Shakespeare." *Ephemera Critica.* London: Archibald Constable, 1901. 351–69.

——. "Shakespeare as a Ladies' Man." *Boudoir* Apr. 1905: 295–302.

Conway, Moncure D. "The Pound of Flesh." *Nineteenth Century* May 1880: 828–39.

Cook, Dutton. *"The Merchant of Venice": Nights at the Play.* London: Chatto and Windus, 1883. 2:223–27.

Crawford, R. F. *Letters and Leaflets on Usury.* London: Crawford, 1889.

C. S. "Mr. Ruskin and Mr. Irving's Shylock." *Theatre* 1 Mar. 1880: 169.

Cunningham, William. *Christian Opinion on Usury.* Edinburgh: Macmillan, 1884.

Dale, R. W. *Genius the Gift of God: A Sermon on the Tercentenary of the Birth of Shakespeare.* London: Hamilton, Adams, 1864.

Davis, Israel. "The Character of Shylock." *Theatre* 1 Dec. 1879: 258–59.

Deane, Anthony C. *His Own Place: The Tercentenary "Shakespeare Sermon."* Holy Trinity Church, Stratford-upon-Avon, 30 Apr. 1916. London: J. Hewetson, 1916.

Dimock, Arthur. "The Conspiracy of Dr. Lopez." *English Historical Review* July 1894: 440–72.

Downing, Charles. *God in Shakespeare.* London: Unwin, 1890.

——. *Messiahship of Shakespeare.* London: Greening, 1901.

Drage, Geoffrey. "Alien Immigration." *Fortnightly Review* Jan.–June 1895: 37–46.

——. "Alien Immigration." *Journal of the Royal Statistical Society* Mar. 1895: 1–30.

Dunraven. "The Invasion of Destitute Aliens." *Nineteenth Century* June 1892: 985–1000.

Dyche, J. A. "The Jewish Immigrant." *Contemporary Review* Mar. 1899: 379–99.

E. R. R. "Ellen Terry as Portia." *Theatre* 1 Jan. 1880: 49.

——. "Henry Irving as Shylock." *Theatre* 1 Jan. 1880: 16.

Eaton, T. R. *Shakespeare and the Bible.* London: Blackwood, 1860.

Eliot, George. "The Modern Hep! Hep! Hep!" *Impressions of Theophrastus Such.* New York: Harper and Brothers, 1879.

Elliott, M. L. *Shakespeare's Garden of Girls.* London: Remington, 1885.

Ellis, Charles. *The Christ in Shakespeare.* London: Houlston, 1897.

——. *Shakspeare and the Bible.* London: Bagster, 1896.

English Association. *The Early Stages in the Teaching of English.* Pamphlet no. 14. Oxford: Oxford UP, 1910.

——. *The Teaching of Shakespeare in Secondary Schools.* Pamphlet no. 2. (frag., n.d.). British Library Catalogue AC 2664.

——. "Types of English Curricula in Boys' Secondary Schools" (frag., n.d.). British Library Catalogue AC 2664.

Evans-Gordon, W. "The Stranger within Our Gates." *Nineteenth Century* Feb. 1911: 210–16.

Farrow, Thomas. *In the Money-Lender's Clutches.* London: Yeoman, 1896.

——. *The Money-Lender Unmasked.* London: Roxburgh, 1895.

Finlay-Johnson, Harriet. *The Dramatic Method of Teaching.* London: Nisbet, 1911.

Firth, C. H. *Sir Sidney Lee, 1859–1926.* From the Proceedings of the British Academy. Vol. 15. London: Humphrey Milford, 1929.

Fox, Stephen N. "The Invasion of Pauper Foreigners." *Contemporary Review* June 1888: 855–67.

Freckelton, T. W. "The Church and the Drama." Sermon, delivered at Bradford, 29 Jan. 1865. London: John Maxwell, 1865.

Furnivall, F. J. "The Character of Shylock." *Theatre* 1 Dec. 1879: 255–56.

Fyfe, H. Hamilton. "The Alien and the Empire." *Nineteenth Century* Sept. 1903: 414–19.

Gasquet, Cardinal F. A. "Shakespeare." I. Gollancz, *Book* 25–29.

Goldie, Junior. *Our Shakespeare Wrote the Bible*. London: Walter Jenn, 1929.

Gollancz, Hermann. "Hebrew Ode." I. Gollancz, *Book* 307–9.

——. *Shakespeare and Rabbinic Thought*. Sermon, delivered at Bayswater Synagogue. 29 Apr. 1916. London: Wertheimer, Lea and Co., 1916.

Gollancz, Israel. "Bits of Timber: Some Observations on Shakespearian Names—'Shylock'; 'Polonius'; 'Malvolio.'" I. Gollancz, *Book* 170–78.

——, ed. *A Book of Homage to Shakespeare*. Oxford: Humphrey Milford, 1916.

Grinfield, Thomas. *Remarks on the Moral Influence of Shakspeare's Plays*. London: Longman, 1850.

Hales, John W. "Shakespeare and the Jews." *English Historical Review* Oct. 1894: 652–61.

——. "Shakespeare and Puritanism." *Contemporary Review* Jan. 1895: 54–67.

Halliwell, J. O. *An Attempt to Discover Which Version of the Bible Was That Ordinarily Used by Shakespeare*. London: Chiswick P, 1867.

Harris, Frank. *The Women of Shakespeare*. London: Methuen, 1911.

Hatton, Joseph. *Henry Irving's Impressions of America*. 2 vols. London: Sampson Low, Marston, Searle, and Rivington, 1884.

Hawkins, Frederick. "The Character of Shylock." *Theatre* 1 Dec. 1879: 260–61.

——. "Shylock and Other Stage Jews." *Theatre* 1 Nov. 1879: 191–98.

Hayward, F. H. *The Primary Curriculum*. London: Ralph, Holland, 1909.

Heard, J. "Why Women Should Study Shakespeare." *Manhattan* 6 June 1884: 620–28.

Herford, C. H. "The Merchant of Venice." *National Home-Reading Union Magazine* 7 Feb. 1898: 71–73.

Hood, E. P. "Sermons from Shakespeare." Clippings from the *Christian Globe* 12 Apr. 1877–79, Aug. 1877. Birmingham Shakespeare Library Collection.

Hutton, W. H. *A Shakespeare Sermon: Preached in the Cathedral Church of Peterborough on the First Sunday after Easter, 1916*. Peterborough Diocesan *Magazine*. Leicester: n.p., 1916. 85–88.

Hyatt, Alpheus. "The Influence of Women in the Evolution of the Human Race." *Natural Science* 8 (1897): 89–93.

Irving, Henry. "The Character of Shylock." *Theatre* 1 Dec. 1879: 254–55.

Jameson, Anna. "Portia." *Characteristics of Women, Moral, Poetical, and Historical*. London: Saunders and Otley, 1833.

Jeyes, S. H. "Foreign Pauper Immigration." A. White, *Destitute* 168–91.

Johnson, Samuel. "Preface to Shakespeare (1765)." *Johnson on Shakespeare*. Ed. Walter Raleigh. Oxford: Oxford UP, 1908.

Jones, Henry A. "Religion and the Stage." *Nineteenth Century* Jan. 1885: 154–69.

Kellett, E. E. "Shakespeare's Amazons." *Suggestions: Literary Essays.* Cambridge: Cambridge UP, 1923.

Kingsley, Charles. "On English Literature." *Literary and General Lectures and Essays.* London: Macmillan, 1890. 245–65.

Knox, E. V. "Did Shakespeare Go to Church?" *Punch* 2 Nov. 1927: 490, 493.

Knox, Kathleen. "On the Study of Shakespeare for Girls." *Journal of Education* Apr. 1895: 222–23.

Laffan, R. S. de C. "Shakespeare, the Prophet" (22 Apr. 1894). Arbuthnot 22–36.

Lee, Sidney. "The Original of Shylock." *Gentleman's Magazine* Feb. 1880: 185–200.

———. "Roderigo Lopez." *Dictionary of National Biography.* London: Smith, Elder, 1909. 132–34.

Leppington, Blanche. "Some Notes on the 'Merchant of Venice' for Beginners." *National Home-Reading Union Magazine* 7 Feb. 1898: 73–74.

Lilly, W. S. "Shakespeare's Protestantism." *Fortnightly Review* June 1904: 966–83.

Luce, Morton. "The Character of Shakespeare." I. Gollancz, *Book* 129–34.

Lyttelton, E. *Give God the Glory. Shakespeare Sermon Preached at Worcester Cathedral on the First Sunday after Easter, 1916.* Eton College: Spottiswoode, Ballantyne, 1916.

Malcolm, W. H. *Shakspere and Holy Writ.* London: Marcus Ward, 1881.

Mangasarian, Mangasar M. *Lord and Lady Macbeth: Sermon.* St. George's Hall: n.p., 1887. N.p.

Marshall, Frank. "The Character of Shylock." *Theatre* 1 Dec. 1879: 256–57.

———. "Introduction." *The Merchant of Venice. The Henry Irving Shakespeare.* Ed. Henry Irving and Frank Marshall. London: Blackie, 1888.

Martin, Helena Faucit. "Portia." 1 Sept. 1880 (for private circulation). British Library Catalogue 11763 cc18.

Martin, Theodore. "The Character of Shylock." *Theatre* 1 Dec. 1879: 253–54.

Mason, E. W. *The Forgotten Teaching and Neglected Discipline of the Church as to Usury.* Leicester: Co-operative Print Society, 1900.

McArthur, W. A. "The Imperial Aspect." A. White, *Destitute* 131–45.

Montefiore, L. G. "Anglo-Jewry at the Cross-roads." *Jewish Review* July 1914: 128–35.

Morley, George. "Shakespeare and the Bible." Articles from *Home Words,* 1905. Birmingham Shakespeare Library Collection.

Morrison, George H. *Christ in Shakespeare.* London: James Clarke, 1928.

Moulton, R. G. "Shakespeare as the Central Point in World Literature." I. Gollancz, *Book* 228–30.

Mr. Henry Irving and Miss Ellen Terry in America: Opinions of the Press. Chicago: Morris, 1884.

M. S. C. "An Old Playgoer on the Modern Theatre." *Theatre* 1 Mar. 1880: 149–51.

Murray, J. B. C. *The History of Usury.* Philadelphia: Lippincott, 1866.

"Museus." "Christ in English Literature." *Contemporary Review.* Literary supp. Jan. 1908: 1–5.

Neale, Francis. *An Essay on Money-Lending.* London: Pickering, 1826.

O'Callaghan, Rev. J. *Usury or Interest Proved to Be Repugnant to the Divine and Ecclesiastical Laws, and Destructive to Civil Society.* London: Clement, 1825.

Oliphant, Margaret. *The Makers of Venice.* London: Macmillan, 1888.

Owen, E. C. E. "English Literature." *The Public Schools from Within: A Collection of Essays on Public School Education* . . . . London: Sampson Low, Marston, 1906. 46–54.

Palmer, Herbert. "Shakespeare Need Not Apply." *English Review* 33 (1921): 473–80.

Pearson, J. B. *On the Theories on Usury* . . . . Cambridge: Deighton, Bell, 1876.

Plumptre, Charles. "The Religion and Morality of Shakespeare's Works." Lecture delivered before the Sunday Lecture Society, 16 Nov. 1873. British Library Catalogue 11761.b.19.

Polkinghorne, R. K., and M. I. R. Polkinghorne. *Modern Teaching: Practical Suggestions for Junior and Senior Schools.* London: Home Library Book, 1928.

Potter, Beatrice. "East London Labour." *Nineteenth Century* Aug. 1888: 161–83.

———. "The Jewish Community." *Life and Labour of the People in London.* Ed. Charles Booth. Vol. 3: *Blocks of Buildings, Schools, and Immigration.* London: Macmillan, 1892. 166–92.

Pownall, Alfred. *Shakspere Weighed in an Even Balance.* London: Saunders, Otley and Co., 1864.

Price, Rev. Thomas. *The Wisdom and Genius of Shakespeare.* London: Adam Scott, 1853.

Procter, William. *Shakespeare and Scripture.* London: H. R. Allenson, 1929.

Prothero, R. E. *The Psalms in Human Life.* London: John Murray, 1903.

Rawnsley, H. D. *Shakespeare: A Tercentenary Sermon.* London: Skeffington, 1916.

Read, F. W. *Evils of State Interference with Money Lending.* London: Watts, 1896.

Reaney, G. S. "The Moral Aspect." A. White, *Destitute* 71–99.

Reed, Haythorne. *A Commentary on the Law Relating to Money-Lenders and the Money-Lenders Act, 1900.* London: Waterlow, 1900.

Reed, Marcus. "Is Portia Possible?" *MacMillan's Magazine* (1906): 375–82.

Replies to Essays and Reviews. Oxford and London: John Henry and James Parker, 1862.

Roberts, A. E., and A. Barter. *The Teaching of English.* London: Blackie, 1908.

Roberts, W. Page. "The Genius of Shakespeare." Shakespeare birthday sermon, 25 Apr. 1915. Reprinted in *Guardian* (Birmingham) 29 Apr. 1915.

Ruskin, John. *The Stones of Venice* (1851). Vol. 1. London: Allen, 1906.

Russell, C., and H. S. Lewis. *The Jew in London: A Study of Racial Character and Present-Day Conditions.* London: Unwin, 1900.

Salmon, Edward. *Juvenile Literature as It Is.* London: Drane, 1888.

——. "What Girls Read." *Nineteenth Century* Oct. 1886: 515–29.

Schloss, David F. "The Jew as a Workman." *Nineteenth Century* Jan. 1891: 96–109.

Selitrenny, L. "The Jewish Working Woman in the East End." *Social Democrat* Sept. 1898: 271–75.

Selkirk, J. B. *Bible Truths with Shakspearian Parallels.* London: Whittaker, 1879.

Shaw, George Bernard. *Dramatic Opinions and Essays.* Vol. 2. New York: Brentano's, 1906–7.

——. *Three Plays for Puritans.* London: Penguin, 1946.

Sillar, R. G. *Her Majesty's Ship Erin in a Gale.* London: Southey, 1881.

——. *Usury: A Paper Read before the London Junior Clergy Society . . . .* London: Southey, 1883.

——. *Usury: A Paper Read before Some Members of the University of Cambridge . . . .* London: Exeter Hall, 1885.

——. *Usury: A Paper Read before the "Somerville Club . . . "* London: Southey, 1883.

Smith, Arnold. *Aims and Methods in the Teaching of English.* London: Constable, 1915.

Smith, Goldwin. "Can Jews Be Patriots?" *Nineteenth Century* May 1878: 875–87.

——. "England's Abandonment of the Protectorate of Turkey." *Contemporary Review* Feb. 1878: 603–19.

——. "The Jewish Question." *Nineteenth Century* Oct. 1881: 494–515.

——. "Shakespeare's Religion and Politics." *Macmillan's Magazine* Nov. 1888: 232–40.

Spedding, James. "The Character of Shylock." *Theatre* 1 Dec. 1879: 257–58.

Spencer, Frederic, ed. *Chapters on the Aims and Practice of Teaching.* Cambridge: Cambridge UP, 1899.

Swinburne, Charles Alfred. *Sacred and Shakespearian Affinities.* London: Bickers, 1890.

The Teaching of English in England. Newbolt Report. London: HMSO, 1921.

Terry, Ellen. *Ellen Terry's Memoirs* (1932). Westport, CT: Greenwood, 1970.

———. "The Triumphant Women." *Four Lectures on Shakespeare.* Ed. Christopher St. John. London: Hopkinson, 1932. 79–122.

Thom, W. T. "Shakespeare Study for American Women." *Shakespeariana* Feb. 1884: 97–102.

Timmins, J. F. *The Poet-Priest: Shakespearian Sermons Compiled for the Use of Students and Public Readers.* London: Blackwood, [1880].

Trench, Richard C. *Every Good Gift from Above: Being a Sermon Preached in the Parish Church of Stratford-upon-Avon on Sunday, April 24, 1864 . . .* London: Macmillan, 1864.

Trench, W. F. "Shakespeare: The Need for Meditation." I. Gollancz, *Book* 135–36.

Tyler, Thomas. "*Shakspere Idolatry.*" N.p.p., 19 Oct. 1888. BM cat. 11763.cc. 18.

Watson, F. B. *Religious and Moral Sentences from Shakespeare Compared with Sacred Passages Drawn from Holy Writ.* London: Calkin and Budd, 1843.

White, Arnold. "Alien Immigration—A Rejoinder." *Fortnightly Review* Mar. 1895: 501–7.

———. "The Invasion of Pauper Foreigners." *Nineteenth Century* Mar. 1888: 414–22.

———. *The Modern Jew.* London: Heinemann, 1899.

———. "The Truth about the Russian Jew." *Contemporary Review* May 1892: 695–708.

———, ed. *The Destitute Alien in Great Britain.* London: Swan Sonnenschein, 1892.

White, Henry Kelsey. "Woman in Shakespeare." *Essays and Poems.* Hull: Tutin, 1907.

Wilson, J. Dover. *Humanism in the Continuation School.* Board of Education Educational Pamphlet no. 43. London: HMSO, 1921.

Wolf, Lucien. *Essays in Jewish History.* Ed. Cecil Roth. London: Jewish Historical Society of England, 1934.

———. "A Jewish View of the Anti-Jewish Agitation." *Nineteenth Century* Feb. 1881: 338–57.

Wordsworth, Charles. "Man's Excellency a Cause of Praise and Thankfulness to God: A Sermon Preached at Stratford-upon-Avon . . . 24 April 1864." Reprinted in Wordsworth, *Knowledge* 381–404.

———. *Shakspeare's Historical Plays.* Vol. 1. Edinburgh and London: William Blackwood, 1883.

———. *Shakspeare's Knowledge and Use of the Bible.* London: Eden, Remington, 1892.

Zangwill, Israel. "The Two Empires." I. Gollancz, *Book* 248.

Zimmern, A. E. "The Aliens Act: A Challenge." *Economic Review* Apr. 1911: 187–97.

SECONDARY SOURCES

Abrahams, Lionel B. "The Condition of the Jews in England at the Time of Their Expulsion in 1290." *Transactions of the Jewish Historical Society of England* 2 (1894–95): 75–105.

——. "The Expulsion of the Jews from England in 1290." *Jewish Quarterly Review* 7 (1895): 75–100, 236–58, 428–50.

Alaya, Flavia. "Victorian Science and the 'Genius' of Woman." *Journal of the History of Ideas* 38 (1977): 61–80.

Alderson, Brian. "Tracts, Rewards and Fairies: The Victorian Contribution to Children's Literature." *Essays in the History of Publishing in Celebration of the 250th Anniversary of the House of Longman, 1724–1974.* Ed. Asa Briggs. London: Longman, 1974. 245–82.

Altholz, J. L. "The Mind of Victorian Orthodoxy: Anglican Responses to 'Essays and Reviews,' 1860–1864." Parsons, *Religion* 4:28–40.

Altick, Richard. *The Cowden Clarkes.* London: Oxford UP, 1948.

——. *The English Common Reader.* Chicago: U of Chicago P, 1957.

Anderson, Benedict. *Imagined Communities.* London: Verso, 1983.

Aronsfeld, C. C. "Jewish Bankers and the Tsar." *Jewish Social Studies* 35 (1973): 87–104.

Ashton, Rosemary. *The German Idea: Four English Writers and the Reception of German Thought, 1800–1860.* Cambridge: Cambridge UP, 1980.

Auerbach, Erich. "Figura" (1944). *Scenes from the Drama of European Literature.* Manchester: Manchester UP, 1984.

——. *Mimesis* (1946). Princeton: Princeton UP, 1953.

Babcock, Robert. *The Genesis of Shakespeare Idolatry, 1766–1799.* Chapel Hill: U of North Carolina P, 1931.

Badawi, M. M. *Coleridge: Critic of Shakespeare.* Cambridge: Cambridge UP, 1973.

Baldick, Chris. *The Social Mission of English Criticism, 1848–1932.* Oxford: Clarendon, 1987.

Barnes, J. H. "'Irving Days' at the Lyceum." *Nineteenth Century* Jan. 1923: 99–116.

Baron, Salo. *The Russian Jew under Tsars and Soviets.* New York: Macmillan, 1964.

Barrell, John. "Coleridge and Shakespeare." Lecture, Sussex University, 1989.

Bartholomew, Michael. "The Moral Critique of Christian Orthodoxy." Parsons, *Religion* 2:166–90.

Bate, Jonathan. *Shakespearean Constitutions.* Oxford: Clarendon, 1989.

Beckett, J. V. *The Aristocracy in England, 1660–1914.* Oxford: Blackwell, 1986.

Beer, John. "Coleridge's Originality as a Critic of Shakespeare." *Studies in the Literary Imagination* 19 (1986): 51–69.

Bermant, Chaim. *The Cousinhood: The Anglo-Jewish Gentry.* London: Eyre and Spottiswood, 1971.

Berry, Ralph. "The Imperial Theme." Foulkes, ed., *Shakespeare* 153–60.

Bingham, Madeleine. *Henry Irving and the Victorian Theatre.* London: Allen and Unwin, 1978.

Black, Eugene C. *The Social Politics of Anglo-Jewry, 1880–1920.* London: Blackwell, 1988.

Bland, Lucy. *Banishing the Beast: English Femininity and Sexual Morality, 1885–1914.* London: Penguin, 1995.

———. "The Married Woman, the 'New Woman' and the Feminist: Sexual Politics of the 1890s." Rendall 141–64.

Bodian, Miriam. "'Men of the Nation': The Shaping of *Converso* Identity in Early Modern Europe." *Past and Present* 143 (1994): 48–76.

Booth, Michael. "Pictorial Acting and Ellen Terry." Foulkes, ed., *Shakespeare* 78–86.

———. *Victorian Spectacular Theatre, 1850–1910.* London: RKP, 1981.

Bowen, John. "Practical Criticism, Critical Practice: I. A. Richards and the Discipline of English." *Literature and History* 13.1 (1987): 77–94.

Bristol, Michael. *Shakespeare's America, America's Shakespeare.* London: Routledge, 1990.

Bristow, Joseph. *Empire Boys.* London: HarperCollins, 1991.

Bromley, J. *The Man of Ten Talents: A Portrait of Richard Chenevix Trench, 1807–86.* London: Society for the Promotion of Christian Knowledge (SPCK), 1959.

Brown, John Russell. "The Realization of Shylock." *Early Shakespeare.* Ed. John Russell Brown and Bernard Harris. London: Arnold, 1961. 187–209.

Brown, Malcolm. "Anglo-Jewish Country Houses from the Resettlement to 1800." *Jewish Historical Society of England Transactions* 28 (1981–82): 20–38.

Buckman, Joseph. *Immigrants and the Class Struggle.* Manchester: Manchester UP, 1983.

Bullough, Geoffrey, ed. *Narrative and Dramatic Sources of Shakespeare.* Vol. 1. London: RKP, 1964.

Burstyn, Joan N. *Victorian Education and the Ideal of Womanhood.* New Brunswick, NJ: Rutgers UP, 1984.

Camplin, Jamie. *The Rise of the Plutocrats: Wealth and Power in Edwardian England.* London: Constable, 1978.

Cannadine, David. "The Context, Performance and Meaning of Ritual: The British Monarchy and the 'Invention of Tradition,' c. 1820–1977." *The Invention of Tradition.* Ed. Eric Hobsbawm and Terence Ranger. Cambridge: Cambridge UP, 1983. 101–64.

———. *The Decline and Fall of the British Aristocracy.* New Haven: Yale UP, 1990.

Carpenter, Humphrey, and Mari Prichard, eds. *Oxford Companion to Children's Literature.* Oxford: Oxford UP, 1984.

Cesarani, David. *The Jewish Chronicle and Anglo-Jewry, 1841–1991.* Cambridge: Cambridge UP, 1994.

——, ed. *The Making of Modern Anglo-Jewry.* Oxford: Blackwell, 1990.

Cheyette, Brian. *Constructions of the Jew in English Literature and Society.* Cambridge: Cambridge UP, 1993.

——. "Hillaire Belloc and the 'Marconi Scandal,' 1900–1914: A Reassessment of the Interactionist Model of Racial Hatred." *The Politics of Marginality: Race, the Radical Right and Minorities in Twentieth Century Britain.* Ed. Tony Kushner and Kenneth Lunn. London: Frank Cass, 1990. 131–42.

——. "Jewish Stereotyping and English Literature, 1875–1920: Towards a Political Analysis." *Traditions of Intolerance: Historical Perspectives on Fascism and Race Discourse in Britain.* Ed. Tony Kushner and Kenneth Lunn. Manchester: Manchester UP, 1989. 12–32.

——. "The Other Self: Anglo-Jewish Fiction and the Representation of Jews in England, 1875–1905." Cesarani, *Making* 97–111.

Colls, Robert, and Philip Dodd, eds. *Englishness: Politics and Culture, 1880–1920.* London: Croom Helm, 1986.

Contreras, Jaime. "Family and Patronage: The Judeo-Converso Minority in Spain." Perry and Cruz 127–45.

Cowen, Anne, and Roger Cowen. *Victorian Jews through British Eyes.* Oxford: Oxford UP, 1986.

Craig, Edward Gordon. *Henry Irving.* London: Dent, 1930.

Cunningham, Hugh. "The Language of Patriotism, 1750–1914." *History Workshop Journal* 12 (1981): 8–33.

Darton, Harvey F. *Children's Books in England.* Cambridge: Cambridge UP, 1982.

Davidoff, Leonore. *The Best Circles.* London: Croom Helm, 1973.

Davies, Tony. "Education, Ideology and Literature." *Red Letters* 7 (n.d.): 4–15.

Davin, Anna. "Imperialism and Motherhood." *History Workshop Journal* 5 (1978): 9–66.

——. "'Mind That You Do as You Are Told': Reading Books for Board School Girls, 1870–1902." *Feminist Review* 3 (1979): 89–98.

Davis, Richard. *The English Rothschilds.* Chapel Hill: U of North Carolina P, 1983.

De Bujanda, Jesus M. "Recent Historiography of the Spanish Inquisition (1977–1988): Balance and Perspective." Perry and Cruz 221–47.

Deelman, Christine. *The Great Shakespeare Jubilee.* London: Michael Joseph, 1964.

Delamont, Sarah. "The Contradictions in Ladies' Education." Delamont and Duffin 134–63.

——. "The Domestic Ideology and Women's Education." Delamont and Duffin 164–87.

Delamont, Sarah, and Lorna Duffin. *The Nineteenth-Century Woman*. London: Croom Helm, 1978.

de Lange, Nicholas. "The Origins of Anti-Semitism: Ancient Evidence and Modern Interpretations." Gilman and Katz 21–37.

Dench, Geoff. *Minorities in the Open Society*. London: RKP, 1986.

Dobson, Michael. *The Making of the National Poet*. Oxford: Clarendon, 1992.

Dobson, R. B. "The Decline and Expulsion of the Medieval Jews of York." *Transactions of the Jewish Historical Society of England* 26 (1979): 34–52.

Doree, Stephen. "The Sassoons of Trent Park." *Heritage*. London: Jewish Research Group of the Edmonton Historical Society, 1982. N.p.

Doyle, Brian. "Against the Tyranny of the Past." *Red Letters* 10 (n.d.) 23–33.

——. *English and Englishness*. London: Routledge, 1989.

——. "The Hidden History of English Studies." *Re-reading English*. Ed. Peter Widdowson. London: Methuen, 1982: 17–31.

Drakakis, John. "Theatre, Ideology, and Institution: Shakespeare and the Roadsweepers." *The Shakespeare Myth*. Ed. Graham Holderness. Manchester: Manchester UP, 1988. 24–41.

Drotner, Kirsten. "Schoolgirls, Madcaps, and Air Aces: English Girls and Their Magazine Reading between the Wars." *Feminist Studies* 9 (1983): 33–52.

Dubnow, S. M. *History of the Jews in Russia and Poland* (1916). Trans. I. Friedlander. Vol. 1. N.p.: Ktav, 1975.

Duffin, Lorna. "Prisoners of Progress: Women and Evolution." Delamont and Duffin 57–91.

Dyhouse, Carol. *Feminism and the Family in England, 1880–1939*. Oxford: Blackwell, 1989.

——. *Girls Growing Up in Late Victorian and Edwardian England*. London: RKP, 1981.

——. "Miss Buss and Miss Beale: Gender and Authority in the History of Education." Hunt, *Lessons* 22–38.

——. "Social Darwinistic Ideas and the Development of Women's Education in England, 1880–1920. *History of Education* 5 (1976): 41–58.

——. "Towards a 'Feminine' Curriculum for English Schoolgirls: The Demands of Ideology, 1870–1963." *Women's Studies International Quarterly* 1 (1978): 297–311.

Eagleton, Terry. *Literary Theory*. Oxford: Blackwell, 1983.

Elman, Peter. "The Economic Causes of the Expulsion of the Jews in 1290." *Economic History Review* 7 (1937): 145–54.

Endelman, Todd. "Communal Solidarity among the Jewish Elite of Victorian London." *Victorian Studies* 28 (1985): 491–526.

——. "The Englishness of Jewish Modernity in England." *Toward Modernity: The European Jewish Model*. Ed. Jacob Katz. New Brunswick, NJ: Transaction, 1987.

——. "German Jews in Victorian England: A Study in Drift and Defection." Frankel and Zipperstein 57–87.

——. "Liberalism, Laissez-Faire, and Anglo-Jewry, 1700–1905." *Contemporary Jewry* (Fall–Winter 1980): 2–12.

——. "Native Jews and Foreign Jews in London, 1870–1914." *The Legacy of Jewish Migration: 1881 and Its Impact.* Ed. David Berger. New York: Brooklyn College P, 1983. 109–29.

——. *Radical Assimilation in English Jewish History, 1656–1945.* Bloomington: Indiana UP, 1990.

Englander, David. "Anglicized Not Anglican: Jews and Judaism in Victorian Britain." Parsons, *Religion* 1:235–73.

Ensor, R. C. K. *England, 1870–1914.* Oxford: Oxford UP, 1966.

Feldman, David. *Englishmen and Jews: Social Relations and Political Culture, 1840–1914.* New Haven: Yale UP, 1994.

——. "The Importance of Being English: Jewish Immigration and the Decay of Liberal England." *Metropolis London.* Ed. David Feldman and Gareth Stedman Jones. London: Routledge, 1989: 56–84.

——. "Jews in London, 1880–1914." *Patriotism: The Making and Unmaking of British National Identity.* Vol. 2: *Minorities and Outsiders.* Ed. Raphael Samuel. London: Routledge, 1989: 207–29.

Felperin, Howard. "Bardolatry Then and Now." Marsden 129–44.

——. *The Uses of the Canon.* Oxford: Clarendon, 1990.

Felsenstein, Frank. *Anti-Semitic Stereotypes.* Baltimore: Johns Hopkins UP, 1995.

Finestein, Israel. "Jewish Emancipationists in Victorian England: Self-Imposed Limits to Assimilation." Frankel and Zipperstein 38–56.

Foakes, R. A. *Coleridge on Shakespeare.* London: RKP, 1971.

Foulkes, Richard. "Helen Faucit and Ellen Terry as Portia." *Theatre Notebook* 31 (1977): 27–37.

——. *The Shakespeare Tercentenary of 1864.* London: Society for Theatre Research, 1984.

——. "The Staging of the Trial Scene in Irving's *The Merchant of Venice.*" *Educational Theatre Journal* 28 (1976): 312–17.

——, ed. *Shakespeare and the Victorian Stage.* Cambridge: Cambridge UP, 1986.

Frankel, Jonathan. "Assimilation and the Jews in Nineteenth-Century Europe: Towards a New Historiography." Frankel and Zipperstein 1–37.

Frankel, Jonathan, and Steven J. Zipperstein. *Assimilation and Community: The Jews in Nineteenth-Century Europe.* Cambridge: Cambridge UP, 1992.

Frei, Hans W. *The Eclipse of Biblical Narrative.* New Haven: Yale UP, 1974.

Friedlander, Gerald. *Shakespeare and the Jew.* London: Routledge, 1921.

Gainer, Bernard. *The Alien Invasion: The Origins of the Aliens Act of 1905.* London: Heinemann, 1972.

Gardner, Juliet. *The New Woman*. London: Collins and Brown, 1993.

Garrard, John. *The English and Immigration, 1880–1910*. London: Oxford UP, 1971.

Gartner, Lloyd P. *The Jewish Immigrant in England, 1870–1914*. London: Simon, 1960.

———. "Notes on the Statistics of Jewish Immigration to England, 1870–1914." *Jewish Social Studies* 22 (1960): 97–102.

Gaye, Freda, Ed. *Who's Who in the Theatre*. London: Pitman, 1967.

Gilam, Abraham. *The Emancipation of the Jews in England, 1830–1860*. New York: Garland, 1982.

Gilman, Sander L. *Difference and Pathology: Stereotypes of Sexuality, Race, and Madness*. Ithaca: Cornell UP, 1985.

———. *Jewish Self-Hatred: Anti-Semitism and the Hidden Language of the Jews*. Baltimore: Johns Hopkins UP, 1986.

———. *The Jew's Body*. New York: Routledge, 1991.

———. *On Blackness without Blacks*. Boston: Hall, 1982.

Gilman, Sander, and Steven Katz, eds. *Anti-Semitism in Times of Crisis*. New York: New York UP, 1991.

Gorham, Deborah. "The Ideology of Femininity and Reading for Girls, 1850–1914." Hunt, *Lessons* 39–59.

———. *The Victorian Girl and the Feminine Ideal*. London: Croom Helm, 1982.

Gould, Stephen Jay. "Science and Jewish Immigration." *Hen's Teeth and Horse's Toes*. London: Penguin, 1983.

Graetz, Heinrich. *History of the Jews* (1894). Vol. 4. Philadelphia: Jewish Publication Society, 1967.

Greenberg, Louis. *The Jews in Russia*. 2 vols. New Haven: Yale UP, 1944–51.

Gross, George C. "Mary Cowden Clarke, 'The Girlhood of Shakespeare's Heroines,' and the Sex Education of Victorian Women." *Victorian Studies* 16 (1972): 37–58.

Gross, John. *Shylock*. London: Chatto and Windus, 1992.

Gwyer, John. "The Case of Dr. Lopez." *Transactions of the Jewish Historical Society of England* 16 (1952): 163–84.

Halliday, F. E. *The Cult of Shakespeare*. London: Duckworth, 1951.

Halliday, R. J. "Social Darwinism: A Definition." *Victorian Studies* 14 (1970–71): 389–405.

Harris, Jonathan Gil. "Ruy Lopez Openings: The Jewish Doctor, the Pathological Body Politic, and *The Whore of Babylon*." MS.

Harrison, J. F. C. *Late Victorian Britain*. London: Fontana, 1990.

Hartman, Geoffrey. "Meaning, Error, Text." *Yale French Studies* 69 (1985): 145–49.

Hartnoll, Phyllis, ed. *Oxford Companion to the Theatre*. Oxford: Oxford UP, 1983.

Henriques, H. S. Q. *The Jews and the English Law*. London: Bibliophile, 1908.

Hichens, Robert. "Irving as Shylock." Saintsbury and Palmer 165–71.

Holcombe, Lee. *Wives and Property*. Oxford: Robertson, 1983.

Hollis, Patricia. "Women in Council: Separate Spheres, Public Space." Rendall 192–213.

Holmes, Colin. "Immigrants, Refugees and Revolutionaries." Slatter 7–22.

———. *John Bull's Island: Immigration and British Society, 1871–1971*. London: Macmillan, 1988.

Holton, Robert. "'A True Bond of Unity': Popular Education and the Foundation of the Discipline of English Literature in England." *Dalhousie Review* 66 (1986): 31–44.

Horstman, Allen. *Victorian Divorce*. London: Croom Helm, 1985.

Hughes, Alan. *Henry Irving, Shakespearean*. Cambridge: Cambridge UP, 1981.

Hunt, Felicity. "Divided Aims: The Educational Implications of Opposing Ideologies in Girls' Secondary Schooling, 1850–1940." Hunt, *Lessons* 3–21.

———, ed. *Lessons for Life: The Schooling of Girls and Women, 1850–1950*. Oxford: Blackwell, 1987.

Irving, Laurence. *Henry Irving*. London: Faber, 1951.

Jackson, Russell. "Before the Shakespeare Revolution: Developments in the Study of Nineteenth-Century Shakespearian Production." *Shakespeare Survey* 35 (1982): 1–12.

Jay, Elisabeth. *Faith and Doubt in Victorian Britain*. London: Macmillan, 1986.

Johnson, Richard. "Educational Policy and Social Control in Early Victorian England." *Past and Present* 49 (1970): 96–119.

———. "Notes on the Schooling of the English Working Class, 1780–1850." *Schooling and Capitalism*. Ed. Roger Dale, Geoff Esland, and Madeleine MacDonald. London: Routledge, 1976. 44–54.

———. "'Really Useful Knowledge': Radical Education and Working-Class Culture, 1790–1848." *Working-Class Culture*. Ed. John Clarke, Chas Critcher, and Richard Johnson. London: Hutchinson, 1979. 75–102.

Jones, Barbara. "The Day Labourer and the Queen." *Grand Street* 7 (1988): 168–75.

Jones, Greta. *Social Darwinism and English Thought*. Brighton: Harvester, 1980.

Jones, Marion. "Stage Costume: Historical Verisimilitude and Stage Convention." Foulkes, ed., *Shakespeare* 56–73.

Jones, Norman. *God and the Moneylenders: Usury and Law in Early Modern England*. Oxford: Blackwell, 1989.

Kadish, Sharman. *Bolsheviks and British Jews*. London: Frank Cass, 1992.

Kamen, Henry. *Inquisition and Society in Spain*. London: Weidenfeld and Nicolson, 1985.

———. "The Mediterranean and the Expulsion of Spanish Jews in 1492." *Past and Present* 119 (1988): 30–55.

———. *The Spanish Inquisition*. London: Weidenfeld and Nicolson, 1965.

Kaplan, Stanley. "The Anglicization of the East European Jewish Immigrant as Seen by the London *Jewish Chronicle*, 1870–1897." *Yivo Annual of Jewish Social Science* 10 (1955): 267–78.

Katz, David. *The Jews in the History of England, 1485–1850*. Oxford: Clarendon, 1994.

———. *Philo-Semitism and the Readmission of the Jews to England, 1603–1655*. Oxford: Clarendon, 1982.

Kaye, Elaine. *A History of Queen's College, London, 1848–1972*. London: Chatto and Windus, 1972.

King, Noel. "'The Teacher Must Exist before the Pupil': *The Newbolt Report on the Teaching of English in England, 1921*." *Literature and History* 13 (1987): 14–37.

Kirschenbaum, Adam. "Jewish and Christian Theories of Usury in the Middle Ages." *Jewish Quarterly Review* 75 (1985): 270–89.

Kleb, William E. "Shakespeare in Tottenham-Street: An 'Aesthetic' *Merchant of Venice*." *Theatre Survey* 16 (1975): 97–121.

Kushner, Tony, ed. *The Jewish Heritage in British History: Englishness and Jewishness*. London: Frank Cass, 1992.

Landa, M. J. *The Jew in Drama*. London: King, 1926.

Landes, David. "The Jewish Merchant: Typology and Stereotypology in Germany." *Leo Baeck Yearbook* 19 (1974): 11–23.

Lawson, John, and Harold Silver. *A Social History of Education in England*. London: Methuen, 1973.

Lazar, Moshe. "The Lamb and the Scapegoat: The Dehumanization of the Jews in Medieval Propaganda Imagery." Gilman and Katz 38–30.

———. "Scorched Parchments and Tortured Memories: The 'Jewishness' of the Anussim (Crypto-Jews)." Perry and Cruz 176–206.

Lea, Henry Charles. *A History of the Inquisition in Spain*. 4 vols. London: Macmillan, 1906–7.

Lewis, Jane. *The Politics of Motherhood*. London: Croom Helm, 1980.

———. *Women in England, 1870–1950*. Brighton: Wheatsheaf, 1984.

Lipman, V. D. *A History of the Jews in Britain since 1858*. Leicester: Leicester UP, 1990.

Loomba, Ania. *Gender, Race, Renaissance Drama*. Manchester: Manchester UP, 1989.

Loughrey, Bryan, and Graham Holderness. "Shakespearean Features." Marsden 183–201.

Lunn, Kenneth, ed. *Hosts, Immigrants, and Minorities: Historical Responses to Newcomers in British Society, 1870–1914*. Folkestone, Kent: Dawson, 1980.

———. "Political Anti-Semitism before 1914: Fascism's Heritage?" *British*

Fascism: Essays on the Radical Right in Inter-War Britain. Ed. Kenneth Lunn and Richard C. Thurlow. London: Croom Helm, 1980. 20–40.

Mackenzie, John M. *Imperialism and Popular Culture.* Manchester: Manchester UP, 1986.

Maclure, Stuart J., ed. *Educational Documents: England and Wales, 1816–1963.* London: Chapman and Hall, 1965.

Marvell, Roger. *Ellen Terry.* London: Heinemann, 1968.

Marks, Lara V. *Model Mothers: Jewish Mothers and Maternity Provision in East London, 1870–1939.* Oxford: Clarendon, 1994.

Marrus, Michael R. "European Jewry and the Politics of Assimilation: Assessment and Reassessment." *Jewish Assimilation in Modern Times.* Ed. Bela Vago. Boulder, CO: Westview, 1981. 5–23.

Marsden, Jean, ed. *The Appropriation of Shakespeare.* Harvester: Hemel Hempstead, 1991.

Maude, Cyril. "Irving as Shylock." Saintsbury and Palmer 171–73.

Menache, Sophie. "Faith, Myth and Politics — the Stereotype of Jews and their Expulsion from England and France." *Jewish Quarterly Review* 75 (1985): 351–74.

Miner, Earl. "Afterword." Miner, *Literary* 370–94.

——, ed. *Literary Uses of Typology.* Princeton: Princeton UP, 1977.

Modder, Frank Montague. *The Jew in the Literature of England to the End of the Nineteenth Century.* Philadelphia: Jewish Publication Society, 1939.

Moore, Edward M. "Henry Irving's Shakespearean Productions." *Theatre Survey* 17 (1976): 195–216.

Moore, James R. "Freethought, Secularism, Agnosticism: The Case of Charles Darwin." Parsons, *Religion* 1:274–319.

Morris, Norman. "State Paternalism and *Laissez-faire* in the 1860s." *Studies in the Government and Control of Education since 1860.* London: Methuen, 1970. 13–26.

Naman, Anne Aresty. *The Jew in the Victorian Novel.* New York: AMS P, 1980.

Odell, George C. *Shakespeare from Betterton to Irving.* Vol. 2. London: Constable, 1920.

Palmer, D. J. *The Rise of English Studies.* London: Oxford UP, 1965.

Panitz, Esther L. *The Alien in Their Midst: Images of Jews in English Literature.* London: Associated UP, 1981.

Parsons, Gerald. "Biblical Criticism in Victorian Britain: From Controversy to Acceptance?" Parsons, *Religion* 2:238–57.

——. "On Speaking Plainly: 'Honest Doubt and the Ethics of Belief.'" Parsons, *Religion* 2:191–219.

——, ed. *Religion in Victorian Britain.* 4 vols. Manchester UP, 1988.

Pederson, Joyce Senders. "The Reform of Women's Secondary and Higher Education: Institutional Change and Social Values in Mid and Late Victorian England." *History of Education Quarterly* (1979): 61–91.

———. "Schoolmistresses and Headmistresses: Elites and Education in Nineteenth Century England." *Journal of British Studies* 15 (1975): 135–62.

Perry, Mary Elizabeth, and Anne J. Cruz. *Cultural Encounters: The Impact of the Inquisition in Spain and the New World*. Berkeley: U of California P, 1991.

Poliakov, Leon. *The History of Anti-Semitism*. Vol. 2. Trans. Natalie Gerardi. London: RKP, 1974.

Pollins, Harold. *Economic History of the Jews in England*. London: Associated UP, 1982.

Pollock, Frederick, and Frederic William Maitland. *The History of English Law before the Time of Edward I*. 2 vols. Cambridge: Cambridge UP, 1895.

Poovey, Mary. *Uneven Developments: The Ideological Work of Gender in Mid-Victorian England*. London: Virago, 1989.

Porter, Bernard. "The British Government and Political Refugees, c. 1880–1914. Slatter 23–45.

Preyer, Robert. *Bentham, Coleridge, and the Science of History*. Bochum-Langendreer: Verlag Heinrich Poppinghaus, 1958.

Prickett, Stephen. "Romantics and Victorians: From Typology to Symbolism." *Reading the Text: Biblical Criticism and Literary Theory*. Ed. Stephen Prickett. Oxford: Blackwell, 1991. 181–224.

Pullan, Brian. *The Jews of Europe and the Inquisition of Venice, 1550–1670*. Oxford: Blackwell, 1983.

Purvis, June. "Social Class, Education and Ideals of Femininity in the Nineteenth Century." *Gender and the Politics of Schooling*. Ed. Madeleine Arnot and Gaby Weiner. London: Open U, 1987. 254–75.

———. "Towards a History of Women's Education in Nineteenth Century Britain: A Sociological Analysis." *Westminster Studies in Education* 4 (1981): 45–79.

Ragussis, Michael. *Figures of Conversion: The Jewish Question and English National Identity*. Durham: Duke UP, 1995.

Rendall, Jane, ed. *Equal or Different: Women's Politics, 1800–1914*. Oxford: Blackwell, 1987.

Reynolds, Kimberley. *Girls Only? Gender and Popular Children's Fiction in Britain, 1880–1910*. London: Harvester, 1990.

Rich, Eric. *The Education Act 1870: A Study of Public Opinion*. London: Longman, 1970.

Rogers, James Allen. "Darwinism and Social Darwinism." *Journal of the History of Ideas* 33 (1972): 265–80.

Rogerson, John. *Old Testament Criticism in the Nineteenth Century*. London: SPCK, 1984.

Rollin, A. R. "Russo-Jewish Immigrants in England before 1881." *Transactions of the Jewish Historical Society of England* 21 (1968): 202–13.

Rose, Jacqueline. *The Case of Peter Pan or the Impossibility of Children's Fiction*. London: Macmillan, 1984.

Roth, Cecil. *A History of the Marranos.* New York: Meridian, 1959.

Rowell, George. *Theatre in the Age of Irving.* Oxford: Blackwell, 1981.

——, ed. *Victorian Dramatic Criticism.* Selected and introduced by George Rowell. London: Methuen, 1971.

Rozmovits, Linda. "*The Wolf and the Lamb:* An Image and Its Afterlife." *Art History* 18.1 (1995): 97–111.

Rubens, Alfred. "The Rothschilds in Caricature." *Transactions of the Jewish Historical Society of England* 20 (1968–69): 76–87.

Rubinstein, W. D. "Education and the Social Origins of the British Elites, 1880–1970." *Past and Present* 112 (1986): 163–207.

——. "Jews among Top British Wealth Holders, 1857–1969: Decline of the Golden Age." *Jewish Social Studies* 34 (1972): 73–84.

——. *Men of Property.* London: Croom Helm, 1981.

——. "Wealth, Elites and the Class Structure of Modern Britain." *Past and Present* 76 (1977): 99–126.

Saintsbury, H. A., and Cecil Palmer, eds. *We Saw Him Act: A Symposium on the Art of Henry Irving.* London: Hurst and Blackett, 1939.

Salbstein, M. C. N. *The Emancipation of the Jews in Britain: The Question of the Admission of Jews to Parliament, 1828–1860.* East Brunswick, NJ: Associated UP, 1982.

Sanderson, Michael. *Education, Economic Change and Society in England, 1780–1870.* London: Macmillan, 1983.

Sartre, Jean-Paul. *Anti-Semite and Jew* (1946). Trans. George J. Becker. New York: Schocken, 1970.

Scholem, Gershom. "Toward an Understanding of the Messianic Idea in Judaism." *The Messianic Idea in Judaism.* London: Unwin, 1971. 1–36.

Scult, Mel. *Millennial Expectations and Jewish Liberties.* Leiden: Brill, 1978.

Segal, Elizabeth. "'As the Twig Is Bent . . . ': Gender and Childhood Reading." *Gender and Reading.* Ed. Elizabeth A. Flynn and Patrocinio P. Schweickart. Baltimore: Johns Hopkins UP, 1986. 165–86.

Shaffer, E. S. *"Kubla Khan" and the Fall of Jerusalem: The Mythological School in Biblical Criticism and Secular Literature, 1770–1880.* Cambridge: Cambridge UP, 1975.

Shanley, Mary Lyndon. *Feminism, Marriage, and the Law in Victorian England, 1850–1895.* London: Tauris, 1989.

Shaw, George Bernard. *The Complete Prefaces.* Vol. 1: *1889–1913.* Ed. Dan H. Laurence and Daniel J. Leary. London: Penguin, 1993.

Shayer, David. *The Teaching of English in Schools, 1900–1970.* London: RKP, 1972.

Shaztmiller, Joseph. *Shylock Reconsidered: Jews, Moneylending and Medieval Society.* Berkeley: U of California P, 1990.

Shell, Marc. "Marranos (Pigs), or From Coexistence to Toleration." *Critical Inquiry* 17 (1991): 306–35.

Silver, Harold. *Education as History*. London: Methuen, 1983.

Slatter, John, ed. *From the Other Shore: Russian Political Emigrants in Britain, 1880–1917*. London: Frank Cass, 1984.

Sprague, A. C. "Irving as Shylock." *Shakespearian Players and Performances*. London: Black, 1954.

———. *'The Merchant of Venice.' Shakespeare and the Actors: The Stage Business in His Plays (1660–1905)*. Cambridge: Harvard UP, 1945. 19–31.

Stanislawski, Michael. *Tsar Nicholas I and the Jews: The Transformation of Jewish Society in Russia, 1825–1855*. Philadelphia: Jewish Publication Society, 1983.

Steedman, Carolyn. "'The Mother Made Conscious': The Historical Development of a Primary School Pedagogy." *History Workshop Journal* 20 (1985): 149–63.

Stetson, Dorothy M. *A Woman's Issue: The Politics of Family Law Reform in England*. Westport, CT: Greenwood, 1982.

Stochholm, Johanne. *Garrick's Folly: The Shakespeare Jubilee of 1769 at Stratford and Drury Lane*. London: Methuen, 1964.

Summers, Anne. "A Home from Home: Women's Philanthropic Work in the Nineteenth Century." *Fit Work for Women*. Ed. Sandra Burman. London: Croom Helm, 1979. 33–63.

Taylor, George. "Shakespearean Interpretation." *Players and Performances in the Victorian Theatre*. Manchester: Manchester UP, 1989. 173–91.

Thompson, Dorothy. "Women, Work and Politics in Nineteenth-Century England: The Problem of Authority." Rendall 57–81.

Thomson, Peter. "'Weirdness That Lifts and Colours All': The Secret Self of Henry Irving." Foulkes, ed., *Shakespeare* 97–105.

Tinkler, Penny. "Learning through Leisure: Feminine Ideology in Girls' Magazines, 1920–50." Hunt, *Lessons* 60–79.

Turnbull, Annmarie. "Learning Her Womanly Work: The Elementary School Curriculum, 1870–1914." Hunt, *Lessons* 83–100.

Vicinus, Martha, ed. *A Widening Sphere: Changing Roles of Victorian Women*. London: Methuen, 1980.

Vickers, Brian. "The Emergence of Character Criticism." *Shakespeare Survey* 34 (1981): 11–21.

Viswanathan, Gauri. "The Beginnings of English Literary Study in British India. *Oxford Literary Review* 9 (1987): 2–26.

Walkley, A. B. "Henry Irving" (1892). Rowell, *Victorian* 134–37.

Weeks, Jeffrey. *Sex, Politics and Society: The Regulation of Sexuality since 1800*. London: Longman, 1981.

Wells, Stanley, and T. J. B. Spencer. "Shakespeare in Celebration, 1564–1964." Ed. T. J. B. Spencer. London: Penguin, 1964. 114–32.

West, Shearer. "The Construction of Racial Type: Caricature, Ethnography, and Jewish Physiognomy in Fin-de-Siècle Melodrama." *Nineteenth Century Theatre* 21.1 (1993): 4–40.

White, Jerry. *Rothschild Buildings: Life in an East End Tenement Block, 1887–1920.* London: RKP, 1980.

Wiener, Martin J. *English Culture and the Decline of the Industrial Spirit, 1850–1980.* London: Penguin, 1992.

Williams, Bill. "The Anti-Semitism of Tolerance: Middle-Class Manchester and the Jews, 1870–1900." *City, Class and Culture: Studies of Social Policy and Cultural Production in Victorian Manchester.* Ed. Alan J. Kidd and K. W. Roberts. Manchester: Manchester UP, 1985. 74–102.

Williams, Raymond. "Social Darwinism." *Problems in Materialism and Culture.* London: New Left, 1980. 86–102.

Winter, William. *Shakespeare on the Stage.* London: Unwin, 1912.

Wolff, Janet. "The Culture of Separate Spheres: The Role of Culture in Nineteenth-Century Public and Private Life." *The Culture of Capital: Art, Power and the Nineteenth Century Middle Class.* Ed. Janet Wolff and John Seed. Manchester: Manchester UP, 1988. 117–34.

Wolpe, Ann Marie. "Education and the Sexual Division of Labour." *Feminism and Materialism.* Ed. Annette Kuhn and Ann Marie Wolpe. London: RKP, 1978. 290–328.

———. "The Official Ideology of Education for Girls." *Educability, Schools and Ideology.* Ed. Michael Flude and John Ahier. London: Croom Helm, 1974. 138–59.

Yovel, Yirmiyahu. *Spinoza and Other Heretics: The Marrano of Reason.* Princeton: Princeton UP, 1989.

Zagorin, Perez. *Ways of Lying: Dissimulation, Persecution, and Conformity in Early Modern Europe.* Cambridge: Harvard UP, 1990.

Index

anti-feminism, 3, 5, 32–34, 49–51. *See*
   also feminism
anti-semitism, Victorian, 9

bardolatry, 9, 11–12, 13, 19
Bentham, Jeremy, 108–10
Bible, changing status of, 19–20,
   23–24
Board of Education, 2
Bradford, E. E., "Manners Makyth
   Man," 122–25
Browne, Rev. G. F., 17

capitalism, Victorian, 104, 107,
   115–17
Carlyle, Thomas, 19
Chesterton, G. K., 56–57
children's literature, Victorian, 100,
   101, 122–25
citizenship, Jewish, 7
civic maternalism, 5, 34, 57
Coke, Sir Edward, 82
Coleridge, Samuel Taylor, 19
   account of Shakespeare, 21–22
Cowden Clarke, Charles, 41, 42, 43,
   47
Cowden Clarke, Mary, 31, 41–47
   Complete Concordance to
     Shakespeare, 43–44
   The Girlhood of Shakespeare's Hero-
     ines, 43, 44–47

"Portia: The Heiress of Belmont,"
   46–47
"Shakespeare as the Girl's Friend,"
   31, 36–37, 42, 49
"The Thane's Daughter," 45
cultural history, 7–8
curriculum, modern, 4, 5

Dale, R. W., 17
Downing, Charles, 25, 28

Earle, John, 107–8, 127
education
   colonial, 4
   female, 4, 5
   and Shakespeare, 34–35, 38–42
   reform, 3–4, 100
   working-class, 4
Education Act (1870), 100
Eliot, George, 19
Ellis, Charles, 25, 28
English Association, 2
English literature, study of, 4
Essex, Earl of, 82

Farrow, Thomas, 111
femininity, Victorian, 5
feminism, 3, 5, 32–34, 45, 51, 69, 72.
   See also anti-feminism
Furnivall, F. J., 92

Library of Congress Cataloging-in-Publication Data

Rozmovits, Linda.

    Shakespeare and the politics of culture in late Victorian England /
Linda Rozmovits.

       p. cm.

    Includes bibliographical references (p.) and index.

    ISBN 0-8018-5836-4 (alk. paper)

      1. Shakespeare, William, 1564–1616. Merchant of Venice.

  2. Literature and society—England—History—19th century.

  3. Shakespeare, William, 1564–1616—Appreciation—England.

  4. Shakespeare, William, 1564–1616—Political and social views.

  5. Great Britain—History—Victoria, 1837–1901. 6. Women in
literature. 7. Jews in literature. I. Title.

PR2825.R69   1998

822.3′3—dc21
                                                97-49966

                                                  CIP

Shakespeare and the Politics of Culture in Late Victorian England
Linda Rozmovits

For today's lovers of Shakespeare, *Hamlet, The Tempest,* and *King Lear* signal the incomparable vision of the bard. But a century ago it was *The Merchant of Venice*, more than any other Shakespearean play, that captured the popular imagination. Heralded as one of Shakespeare's greatest achievements, the play was enshrined in the school curriculum, widely discussed in the popular and scholarly press, and performed as a long-running smash hit on the London stage.

In *Shakespeare and the Politics of Culture in Late Victorian England,* Linda Rozmovits considers how and why *The Merchant of Venice* came to exercise such a powerful hold on late Victorian society. From debates about Portia and the politics of the New Woman to emerging concerns about the changing nature of citizenship, capital, and the longstanding "Jewish question," *The Merchant of Venice* served as a lens through which people filtered their experience of social life and social change. The relationship between the play and the people who studied it, read it, and watched it being performed was extraordinarily dynamic, and it is the nature of this strange and dynamic relationship that this book explores.

LINDA ROZMOVITS is a lecturer in the Department of Cultural Studies at the University of East London.